"A counterintuitively hopeful a
journeys in and out of menta
to manage the illness, *What I Remember of the Little I Understand*
invites us to witness first-hand the harshest of soul-grinding mental afflictions. Underscoring just how crucial for the healing of the mind is the healing also of body, soul, and memory, Erin Grimm searches doggedly for Christ throughout her journeys. Her quest ultimately builds her and her reader up in faith, hope, and love."

—**KATHRYN GREENE-MCCREIGHT**, author
of *Darkness Is My Only Companion*

"With both stark honesty and gentle humility, Erin Grimm invites us into the long journey of healing and hope for those dealing with trauma and mental illness. Her prose is equally honest, articulate, and accessible leaning into her own journey of ongoing healing and life. Grimm's story is a helpful window both for those whose families struggle with mental illness and those who desire to be friends, advocates, and pastors to them."

—**BRENT PETERSON**, co-author of *The Back Side of the Cross*

"Erin Grimm takes us on an inner, insightful odyssey of her own neuroatypicality. Impacted by schizoaffective disorder, she informs us that 'people with psychosis are great teachers of the human condition.' This book, as an emic, psychological translation, is unapologetic, candid, courageous, arresting, and informative as it opens our eyes to a reality that most will never experience and rarely understand."

—**PETER BELLINI**, author of *Truth Therapy*

"Erin Grimm has written a moving, honest, and sometimes painful memoir from the perspective of a person living with mental illness. She outlines in vivid prose the struggles she has faced in her relationships, faith, and career. Yet she also strikes a hopeful note as she describes the process of learning to manage her mental health, maintain fulfilling relationships, and rediscover purpose in life."

—DAVID F. WATSON, professor of New Testament, United Theological Seminary

"Erin Grimm's book is a gift to those who struggle with mental illness. Her willingness to be open about her journey with schizoaffective disorder should embolden others with mental illness to share openly. Sprinkled with passages from scripture and The Book of Common Prayer, this book offers 'breadcrumbs' of hope to those who are blindly navigating the ravages of mental illness—a hope of experiencing true love and full identity in the Triune God."

—CINDY STRONG, education librarian, Seattle Pacific University

What I Remember of the Little I Understand

What I Remember of the Little I Understand

A Memoir of Finding Mental Health in Christ

ERIN GRIMM

Foreword by
Joycelynn Baker and Gwen Benedict

Afterword by
Brent Peterson

RESOURCE *Publications* · Eugene, Oregon

WHAT I REMEMBER OF THE LITTLE I UNDERSTAND
A Memoir of Finding Mental Health in Christ

Resource Publications
An Imprint of Wipf and Stock Publishers
199 W. 8th Ave., Suite 3
Eugene, OR 97401

www.wipfandstock.com

PAPERBACK ISBN: 978-1-6667-7542-6
HARDCOVER ISBN: 978-1-6667-7543-3
EBOOK ISBN: 978-1-6667-7544-0

06/26/23

This book is for Chad Crooks and AJ Braun, my spiritual brothers.
May you and your legacies be a blessing.

Surely you don't disbelieve the prophecies, because you had a hand in bringing them about yourself? You don't really suppose, do you, that all your adventures and escapes were managed by mere luck, just for your sole benefit?

—GANDALF TO MR. BILBO BAGGINS, *THE HOBBIT*

Contents

Contents

Foreword

A GEN-Z PERSPECTIVE

"So how do you want to learn French?" Erin said to me on Zoom, me, in the courtyard of my mother's apartment in Chicago and she, in the bedroom of her house in Seattle. I was nineteen at the time. It was the first time someone asked me *how* I wanted to learn something, instead of *what* I wanted to learn. I told her I didn't know, because I didn't, and with warm enthusiasm she suggested we start with books that I liked. She asked me what books interested me, and I told her, and we planned for the next week. Upon opening the laptop to Zoom with her again, we started our first passage of our favorite book, *The Brothers Karamazov*, both wholly grinning in excitement.

That's the kind of freedom that arises in this book for me as I read it. Erin's focus with others has always hinged on desire and the provocation of desire in others, so that they would be maximally happy with themselves.

The nature of this book is open-ended, never assuming to have all the answers to the challenges that arise in life. A raw honesty burns in these pages, one that is different from the self-help books known to provide such dishonesty. The book is founded on humility: "I reflect on this not with pride . . . ," she writes, "I don't share to brag . . . ," "I still don't know to this day . . ." A constant self-reflective and tempered measure of authority dominates the work and leaves the reader talked with, not at.

The application of Scripture and *The Book of Common Prayer* to the narrative of the book is crucial in *What I Remember of the*

Little I Understand. The stabilizing truth of God's word contrasts heavily and effectively with preceding descriptions of despair. Hope is essential to the balance and life-giving depiction of the human condition.

As an African American woman who has struggled with similarly challenging questions, this book has proven to be a direct testament to the vulnerable and yearning nature of mental illness. The book desires to meet people with kindness, inviting them into the process of slow, but true healing. The book calls forth the sobriety of its readers. Erin appeals to hope, and offers it to those who expect to receive little to none in this lifetime as inhabitants of an unaccepting world.

What I Remember of the Little I Understand couldn't be more timely. In a post-COVID world, where mental illness stands as the conquering cruel strongman of the young adult population, Erin stands prophetically, speaking to her younger and older counterparts with boldness and strength. I have learned things about Erin that I had never known as I read these pages, and I am pleased to be able to relate to her still more. Hope extends to the reader in these pages. Hope that breathes and rests.

Joycelynn Baker
Seattle, Washington
May 9, 2023

AN ELDER'S PERSPECTIVE

I NEEDED TO LET go, release, the story that I continued to relive over and over again.

But first I had to face that little girl who did not know how to speak up. Who felt the pain and fear and then was confused. She stuffed it down. and just relived the nightmares for thirty years. That is, until a counselor with compassion walked her through the dream. It was not just the dark shadow in the doorway but the whole event.

Then came the anger.

But in holding the anger I was still holding the fear. Replaying the story so I would not be molested again. I created another girl. One who would be in control at all times.

It was just another way of telling the same story.

I have walked into my life as a guard version of someone else for far too long, guarded and in control.

At thirty-three years old, I started my meditation practice. Exploring my relationship with Spirit, God, Creator . . . Who was this presence in my life?

Through this process, I found an inner peace with myself and with my God. I felt it clearly when my dad passed away, I deeply felt God and dad's presence then and now. So I knew there was a holy presence that we too can experience here on earth. But to change such a deep-set pattern, I had to work daily at it.

Now again still thirty years after *that*, I walk on the beach near my home. The stormy waves are gone. The Salish Sea is at peace. I take in the smell of the air. I reach down and dip my hand in the sea. I don't want to try and control anymore. Right now, I feel the peace, just like this expansive sea in front of me.

In hopes of healing, I extend a hand toward that little girl I had left behind. I look into her eyes and tell her what no one else has. That she is perfect and that she is safe, and that she is going to be okay.

"People do hurtful and confusing things out of their own pain. He only came once and you are safe now. The dreams are gone," I tell her.

She puts her hand in mine and simply says, "I forgive you."

I see now how strong she is.

From here on out, I will open my eyes and ears and, most of all, my heart. I make a promise to live my life with authenticity and truth.

I will restore my nervous system that was gripped in fear, with faith and love. Shedding light on suffering brings us out of the darkness. Along with that suffering I also find hope and compassion for her and myself and, also, the man, the stranger, who started this whole story.

So I choose hope. She still has it. That little girl inside, or should I call her my soul. We step firmly forward into the new path we will walk together, knowing full well that even if we encounter storms, we will weather them together. With hope, joy, strength, and love.

As I walk this new path, I remember that God is already there and always has been.

Gwen Benedict
Seahurst, Washington
April 18, 2023

Preface

Almighty God, you proclaim your truth
in every age by many voices:
Direct, in our time, we pray, those who speak
where many listen and write what many read;
That they may do their part in making the heart of this people wise,
Its mind sound, and its will righteous;
to the honor of Jesus Christ our LORD. Amen.

—*THE BOOK OF COMMON PRAYER*

I STILL REMEMBER: *I have just run into the ER unadmitted, shouting that everyone knew I had been raped. I am in a hospital room with windows facing into the ER when they ask me to undress. They have locked me up with an attendant and guards and have told me to take off my clothes so they can put me in a straitjacket and give me an antipsychotic medication in my upper thigh—Haldol.*

"Can you close the blinds before I change?"

I am out of my mind, and yet not without a sense of modesty. The woman attendant, visibly startled and probably fearful, draws the blinds closed and averts her eyes. To her, it is as if I am not fully human: You mean psychotic people still have an impulse to modesty?

Three men tie me down after I take off my clothes, and they give me an injection in my upper thigh.

xiii

I feel wrongly persecuted and assaulted, and strain with all my might against their inherent, male strength.

"You should be ashamed of yourselves!"

"Especially you!" I say, looking at a Black attendant as he puts his hands on my groin to stabilize me and administer the injection. If anyone should protect me it would be him since I'm so passionate about civil rights. Instead, he's helped tie me down. My Judas.

His betrayal was incomprehensible—a stranger's betrayal—and from the outside I looked like just one more racist white woman, telling a Black man doing his job in the emergency room with two white men beside him, that he should be ashamed.

AN ORIGINAL COUPLET

To become whole, realize that you already are. Whole.
You are already whole. Holy. And beloved.

Acknowledgments

THANK YOU TO TODD, my husband, whose dedication at work and home ensures that I have time to devote to writing and establishing the proceeds to go directly to charity. The royalties for this book are established so that they are automatically routed to NNU and NTS in support of women clergy and women in leadership. The traumas and joys shared with my readers in this book are not only mine, but they also belong to you. Thank you for graciously supporting me as I wrote this book and for your partnership as I share my life with others so openly as a writer and speaker.

Thank you to Ross Tangedal and Caleb Shupe for your attentive editing work on the final manuscript and for your encouragement during the writing process.

Thank you to my mother and brother for allowing me to publish this honest work and for your loving support. Thank you to my father for providing for us when we were growing up and for reforming your ways so we can have a healthy relationship now, and to my stepmother for taking care of Dad. Thanks also to my in-laws, who have modeled familial health and love for me and my husband since I was fifteen years old.

Thank you to my publisher, who lovingly supported me as I changed this book from psychological thriller, which would probably have sold many more copies, into a supportive and encouraging, though also frank, selective memoir, which, I pray, will help people who suffer rather than entertain those who don't. Thank you, in particular, Matt Wimer, Emily Callihan, George Callihan, Joe Delahanty, Rachel Saunders, and Savanah N. Landerholm.

ACKNOWLEDGMENTS

Thank you, finally, to Nick O'Connell, my teacher at "The Writer's Workshop," a Seattle-based writing program, and Allison Gentry, my fellow student there, for helping me refine chapter 4, which has content from my life that was so traumatic that I hadn't realized I could safely piece it back together without the sky falling in. You brought so much clarity to my very life and with so much love. I don't even know where to begin.

Abbreviations

OLD TESTAMENT

Genesis—Gen
Exodus—Exod
Leviticus—Lev
Numbers—Num
Deuteronomy—Deut
Joshua—Josh
Judges—Judg
Ruth—Ruth
1 Samuel—1 Sam
2 Samuel—2 Sam
1 Kings—1 Kgs
2 Kings—2 Kgs
1 Chronicles—1 Chr
2 Chronicles—2 Chr
Ezra—Ezra
Nehemiah—Neh
Esther—Esth
Job—Job
Psalms—Ps (Pss when citing
    multiple chapters at once)
Proverbs—Prov

Ecclesiastes (or Qoheleth)—
    Eccl (or Qoh)
Song of Solomon—Song
Isaiah—Isa
Jeremiah—Jer
Lamentations—Lam
Ezekiel—Ezek
Daniel—Dan
Hosea—Hos
Joel—Joel
Amos—Amos
Obadiah—Obad
Jonah—Jon
Micah—Mic
Nahum—Nah
Habakkuk—Hab
Zephaniah—Zeph
Haggai—Hag
Zechariah—Zech
Malachi—Mal

NEW TESTAMENT

Matthew—Matt

Mark—Mark

Luke—Luke

John—John

Acts—Acts

Romans—Rom

1 Corinthians—1 Cor

2 Corinthians—2 Cor

Galatians—Gal

Ephesians—Eph

Philippians—Phil

Colossians—Col

1 Thessalonians—1 Thess

2 Thessalonians—2 Thess

1 Timothy—1 Tim

2 Timothy—2 Tim

Titus—Titus

Philemon—Phlm

Hebrews—Heb

James—Jas

1 Peter—1 Pet

2 Peter—2 Pet

1 John—1 John

2 John—2 John

3 John—3 John

Jude—Jude

Revelation—Rev

Introduction

Almighty and eternal God, so draw our hearts to you,
So guide our minds,
So fill our imaginations,
So control our wills,
That we may be wholly yours,
Utterly dedicated unto you;
And then use us, we pray you, as you will,
And always to your glory and the welfare of your people;
Through our LORD and Savior Jesus Christ. Amen.

—*THE BOOK OF COMMON PRAYER*

MY MIND IS LIKE a forest at dawn, a forest through which shafts of light, moments of clarity, sometimes show through wild and free. It is hard sometimes to navigate the darker passages, a condition that is sometimes visible to others. When this happens, people often touch my arm and say my name aloud, several times.

"Erin . . . Erin . . ."

New thoughts rush forward at this prompting, and it is as though I have stepped into a lighter passageway where the sun is as if visible . . . Yet the words have still not made their way to my mouth in reply before I have to turn away a little, ever so slightly, turn away from the brightness of the sun and the shock of another's existence beyond myself.

I rally.

"Yes?" I answer.

Like a deepwater fish brought up to the surface into the sun too quickly, I am as if stunned by this sudden interaction. Another thought drags me back into the darkness of rumination. My breathing becomes shallow.

My husband watches this descent knowingly and then applies pressure to the small of my back. Conversation rushes up again to my lips. Under the pressure of his hand so knowingly applied, clarity will glow for me longer this time.

My prayer while writing this book has been that people of faith, or those interested in becoming people of faith, would be able to focus on hope. However, I also wanted to discourage in myself and in others a blind, wishful-thinking kind of hope. Christ died on a cross, humiliated and rejected. He is there for the abused and the abandoned because he rose again. I live with hope today, but that hasn't always been the case, and I want to share my life as an offering.

When I was a child, I felt abused but thought I wasn't. I didn't have any bruises (or at least not often) or broken bones. But I still had this gaping hole in my soul from emotional and psychological abuse—and I was also physically abused, just without the marks to show for it. I was very inwardly-focused and didn't really analyze family systems in friends or compare. I tended to be a wallflower, while my mom was a social butterfly. She made friends and us kids hung out with one another, her friends' kids and us, me and my little brother. Sometimes her friends' kids bullied me.

Violence was frequent at home, and most often perpetrated against me, the perennial rebel of the family. I was the lightning rod, attracting attention to myself to distract from my parents' marital problems. My little brother, two years younger, absorbed the wreckage into himself. He is a healer and one of my favorite people to talk to when things are rough. Though I was the one who battled with my dad, Mom and my brother still have significant scars.

My father is a good man in many ways, but he struggles with moods and workaholism and he was angry with me throughout my childhood. I think the hardest thing to pinpoint is how someone so affable could also have such a dark streak. A school picture shows the rings of saliva around the neck of my fruit-lined T-shirt collar, a visible reminder of my panicked inner life from a very young age.

Though it has taken many years to rediscover it after focusing acutely on trauma throughout my twenties and early thirties, I am happy to say that I do also have positive memories of childhood. I remember our beautiful garden and Mom walking through the flowerbeds with Birkenstocks, shorts, with hose in hand. I remember the soccer team, which my dad coached lovingly. My brother was in Boy Scouts and my dad was a nurturing presence for him there, too. However, when I think back to my childhood, the thing that sticks out the most are terrifying car rides and head trauma perpetrated by my father.

I was pure-hearted but also irreverent. I often threw things, too. My own temper as a child astounds me—maybe Dad just didn't know how to raise a child with mental illness and brain damage, since I died and was brought back to life when they cut the umbilical cord. I also had thirty seizures a day from ages one through four.

Maybe I inherited his anger.

When I'm feeling particularly vulnerable, I like to tell myself that everything is my fault and that the pain will go away if I just make myself better. This has led to my perfectionism. I'm a recovering perfectionist.

Throughout my high school through college and graduate student years, I read classic literature. By the time I had finished high school I had read all of Tolstoy's works and had read most of Dostoevsky's, much Kafka, and also memorized Shakespearian sonnets for fun. Literature, however, was a means of coping. All I did, *ever*, was read, swim competitively, or flirt with boys (but I was in Christian youth group so I was abstinent through the second year of college, and I got married at twenty-three).

I regulated my mood with music; I was a piano performance major for my two years at Sonoma State. Books also settled me. I was a literature major and have two MAs in literature. The constant mental rupture and anxiety I felt in spite of my calm life after we no longer lived with Dad (he moved out when I was fifteen), and my calm life when I was a college student, played out in my choice of

Romantic music (Chopin, Rachmaninov, and Beethoven) and the intense and frequently violent world of eighteenth- and nineteenth-century European literature, read in the original Spanish, French, German, and Russian.

It regulated my mood and my anxiety perfectly—until it didn't. That's the difference between functional PTSD and unmanageable psychotic illness, an illness which fell upon me when I was twenty-seven to twenty-nine, and with which I still live, though joy, hope, and wellness punctuate my life, thanks to faith, medical help, restored family relationships with good boundaries, and therapy.

A NOTE ON BIBLE TRANSLATION

I use *The Message* as the Bible translation in this book. It is a paraphrase of Scripture, in modern, fresh language.

I did this in my previous work, *Emergent Grace: Christian Hope for Serious Mental Illness*, too.

I cannot tell you how helpful having the *devotional* version has been for my faith since I got burned out, initially, on reading the Bible because it sounded so judgmental in English. Eugene Peterson, the translator, holds your hand through the text and helps you find your footing in the Bible and in the Christian faith in general. He was a pastor and is very pastoral.

PART I

Disintegration

Almighty and everlasting God,
you made the universe with all its marvelous order,
Its atoms, worlds, and galaxies,
And the infinite complexity of living creatures:
Grant that, as we probe the mysteries of your creation,
We may come to know you more truly,
And more surely fulfill our role in your eternal purpose;
In the name of Jesus Christ our LORD. Amen.

—*THE BOOK OF COMMON PRAYER*

IT HAS BEEN SAID that the mind is its own universe, with which I agree. My mind has been on a prickly journey for as long as I can remember. Sometimes my body accompanies the journey of my mind. Sometimes my mind and my body are in radically different places. Since 2015, when I was hospitalized, once involuntarily, my mind and body have been blessedly united by antipsychotic medication, which is essential for me and helps me to thrive and serve God.

To me, advice on how to attend to one's mind given to the mentally ill is aspirational at best. We expect pop-psychology, self-help books, and transformational retreats to help us over the course of a few days to weeks, and for their impacts to last a lifetime. What people tend to leave out as they sell you on materials, seminars, and therapy sessions is that healing, especially healing from psychosis, is a spiral-shaped and lifelong journey. It requires rootedness in something bigger than oneself that will hold all the fragments as you connect the dots, going about your day. For me, this is the role of the Holy Trinity (often referred to as "the divine dance" across the ages) in my life.

There are a lot of theologies of the Holy Trinity. One thing that a lot of them talk about is something called *perichoresis*. This is where Father (or Creator), Son, and Holy Spirit interpenetrate one another, with boundaries, but they are also completely porous. The point is you can't have the Father without the Son and the Holy Spirit; you can't have the Son without the Father and the Holy Spirit; and you can't have the Holy Spirit without the Father and the Son. This reminds me of social mental health as a phenomenon. We are social and faithful creatures, not autonomous individuals, and when we forget this, our mental health and community health suffer. I require constant attention to boundaries, while many don't have to think about such things. But really, we should all think about these things. I like to think my mental health journey has made me more compassionate and more communal, in spite of the paranoia that occasionally leaves me isolated and very worried.

Over time, one learns that restoring the mind is a daily journey that does not have to be a battle. In fact, when we arrive with ourselves one day, looking in the mirror, amazed that our challenges are invisible mental processes rather than physical processes like cancer or so-called "deformities," what's "normal" anyway?, we commit ourselves to being "normal"—just this once. But it's more than this destination of "normalcy," my neuroatypicality. It is a process of *becoming*, only to withdraw and then become, still more, who I always already have been. I have such a rich inner life. This has been alternately exhilarating or terrifying. Sometimes both at once.

I have been reading pop-psychology and self-help books and attending spiritual seminars for a little over a decade. My specific call to them was rooted in the desire to be whole, complete, lacking in nothing. The guides (authors or gurus, pastors or priests) seemed to have arrived. They were to show me the way. The funny thing is that maybe they did understand it all, but it didn't rub off on me because psychosis is a process, a process of disintegration. I enrolled in a seminary in Seattle, determined to study my way to spiritual bliss, only to find that my psychosis kept me from learning amidst hierarchy, from professors who were responsible for grading me, assessing me, judging me. Until very recently, I would rebel and find a way to contradict and undermine, if not shame, authority. I always played it off as mental illness, and it probably was related, but deep down I think that this desire not to be controlled came from the fact that I have a deep inner knowing and wisdom that I am called to share with the world. It points beyond me, to God, through the lens of mental health crises. I think many people with psychosis are great teachers of the human condition and of the interdependent nature of reality. Through a Christian lens, this suggests that we are all dependent on God: psychosis means "a swelling of the psyche," Greek for *soul*.

My desire to contradict and undermine faded after the publication of my first book in early 2023, also with Wipf and Stock Publishers, my favorite publisher. I like to think that this indicates I got a major part of my message "out there." In the current book I share how my message came to be. To this day, however, I ask myself, was it nature or nurture that pulled me to God, to surrender to God, knowing that I will never be whole, complete, and lacking in nothing? Was it nature or nurture that drove me to contradict authority, from parents to professors? By embracing this lack and drive to challenge I have found they are God-shaped. What a relief!

Worship makes me complete—though worship is assuredly not limited to the four walls of a church. It takes place in church, yes, but it is also so much bigger than that for me. Worship, in the image of Mother Mary holding the Christ after his being taken down from the cross—called *La Pietà*, sculpted by Michelangelo—inspires the posture I have taken to cleansing and holding my brain together, with prayer, community, and antipsychotic medication. Like the Virgin holding her beloved son, I hold with an open hand my will, focus, and memory, asking God to cleanse them daily for the sake of my readers and hearers, as well as my friends and family. My mind and my will are an offering to God.

Am I more broken than most? Without my medicine, undoubtedly. And yet with it, my core coheres, much like the Japanese vases that, once broken, are pieced back together with glue containing flecks of gold. There is beauty in breaking if one knows how to attend to the brokenness and build it back stronger, with God at the center. As is written in the book of Ezekiel, we can establish God at the center of our lives forever.

They'll follow my laws and keep my statutes. They'll live in the same land I gave my servant Jacob, the land where your ancestors lived. They and their children and their grandchildren will live there forever, and my servant David will be their prince forever. I'll make a covenant of peace with them that will hold everything together, an everlasting covenant. I'll make them secure and place my holy place

of worship at the center of their lives forever. I'll live right there with them. I'll be their God! They'll be my people!

The nations will realize that I, God, make Israel holy when my holy place of worship is established at the center of their lives forever.

—Ezek 37:24–28

1

Why I Wrote This Book

Direct us, O LORD,
in all our doings with your most gracious favor,
And further us with your continual help;
That in all our works begun, continued, and ended in you,
We may glorify your holy Name, and finally, by your mercy,
Obtain everlasting life; through Jesus Christ our LORD. Amen.

—*THE BOOK OF COMMON PRAYER*

SEVERAL YEARS AGO, I went to the cemetery to visit my grand-mother who is buried there. It is a nice little Catholic cemetery in the outskirts of Sacramento named Calvary Catholic Cemetery. To get there, you drive down a road that parallels I-80 for a couple of minutes, with I-80 on your left and rolling green hills to your right; eventually, gravestones can be seen dotting the hills. Upon enter-ing the gated driveway, there is a tree under which Oma—German for Grandma—is buried next to her husband, my Grandpa Henry. Grandpa Henry was a TV repairman, who paid for all of his siblings' college without ever going himself. He lived with PTSD and, though also known in our family for his anger, he possessed the deep and rare virtue of selflessness, just like his son (my father) today.

PART I: DISINTEGRATION

I don't go to Calvary Catholic often, but felt called to for some reason that day in late 2017. My Aunt Diane is buried there as well. I walked across the street that divided mother and daughter to find my Aunt Diane's gravestone. I have no memories of her, but I am told that she held me when I was small enough to fit in the crook of an adult's arm. She died shortly after I was born. I looked at her tombstone and, as I looked, I realized that Aunt Diane died when she was thirty-four. I visited her that day when I was thirty-two. It occurred to me then how very short life is, and that, as one poem puts it, she had traveled through the night with her own dreams and aspirations that were cut short before her time. She died of breast cancer, with a child, husband, and family left behind to grieve her loss.

I stood at Aunt Diane's grave site, feeling her presence with me. I often feel the presence of spirits about me, even on significant amounts of medicine. I felt her presence and her urging, and it was different from the urging you experience when you are full of life and young; it was the urging of youth suddenly lost and perspectives of surrounding family and friends radically shifted. And I felt like I could understand her for once.

You see, when we are alive, we are run by a different set of rules than when we have died. When we are alive, we take part in competition, ambition. We may or may not have a lot of pride in what we do. Most likely we do or we wouldn't be doing it. We want to appear strong, successful . . . and so we do. All these sorts of things are natural and not to be avoided. Everything unfolds in due time as we progress toward old age.

Have you ever seen a person who was old and uncomfortable about their age? I don't know if it's an American thing, but I have definitely seen people who are ill at ease as they mature into old age. I believe that this is because some of us suffer in old age, not used to a life without ambition.

I like to imagine that, should I be able to live long enough, in my old age I will be mature and at peace with the wrinkles, jiggles, and gray. I like to believe that I will have matured into old age rather than avoiding it. That I will have really lived into the richness of life. I have seen this in a select few, a maturity, wisdom, and grace that none of us can parallel at any stage of our lives other than old age. So rare is it to find a mature person who has matured into their maturity. I focus on the word "mature" here because I find that this maturation process is short-circuited in our society. Maturity requires growing pains, and we often like to hide them away.

On that day, at thirty-two, I myself was in many ways still a child. And yet due to my suffering in early years I also felt a tinge of the maturity of which I speak. Specifically, like the old people I most admire, I was no longer ashamed of who I was. To this day, it's not even a refusal to be ashamed. It just is: I am not ashamed.

Not everyone lives into old age. While some of us die suddenly, others of us do not. My Aunt Diane died slowly after a long fight with cancer; my former neighbor fought cancer and survived and is now thriving. It is a mystery why some of us survive and others don't. But it is a progressive responsibility for those of us who survive to swallow our pride and speak out on behalf of those who lost their battle. Especially in the case of mental illness.

The truth is that some of us, though very much alive in body, are dying in a different way. Some of us, numbed by this experience of feeling dead or panicky inside, may get to the point of even killing ourselves.[1] My life, which I love and cherish, was almost lost in 2015 to psychosis. My life has changed as a result of illness, and yet I am at peace with what only my former self would have called lesser ambitions and, furthermore, I have become a published author.

In writing this now, I can visualize a younger version of myself reading this and thinking that I have settled. This book is not about settling, I must tell you. I live in submission to the illness, having learned that to fight it is to fight yourself, and that it severely worsens your state—at least my illness is this way. Everyone is different. I dance with my illness; I lay it down to bed before laying myself down to bed and it, over time, has become my spiritual path. My personal intention has been to shine through it rather than in spite of it. Please know it is natural to feel anger as you read this

---

1. Call, text, or chat 988 Suicide and Crisis Lifeline if you are experiencing thoughts of suicide. They really helped me and are available 24-7. You matter. Do not kill yourself.

paragraph—I am only talking about myself, and your path may be different. Everyone is different.

Human beings are often struck with illnesses that won't go away, but no matter how much we may suffer at any given time, feelings aren't forever. Mental illness is just one of the many afflictions that a person may suffer from over the course of a life. To suffer is human. To want to survive is human and essential. But the challenge with serious mental struggles is this: can one arrange one's mental furniture fast enough when struck with a devastating diagnosis to survive past our teens and twenties—when most mental illnesses develop—into a vigorous maturity that only the initiated will experience?

Because what I suffer from is a mental illness, schizoaffective disorder, I have had to borrow insights from my deceased aunt to bring myself to write this book because it is unlikely that I will die in my thirties. It is unusual for a thirty-something-year-old to write a book about her life with an illness that has devastated her, disrupted her career trajectory, made it likely that she will never bear children, and almost cost her her marriage. This is not the sort of thing that one usually broadcasts, especially when still young and trying to get ahead in the world. But my aunt and the memory of my aunt persist and have beckoned me to write as if I had died about the process by which I came to cherish my life and my mind and live with great hope.

Unlike many books I've read about mental illness, I'm not writing from a tenured position that protects me from "disgrace"—whatever that is—but from the position of a human being who won't use her profession as a defense for her personhood. Unlike other books I've read, I am not going to write about how I now live without medication, as if it were some badge that, once worn, delivers us from our status of otherwise lacking worth and being human. I'm happy for the people who don't need medication, but the fact is I do require medication, just as a diabetic requires insulin.

Yet this book also is not a "take your meds" book. Although there's more to it than just the reminder to take your meds, my first book could be described, in part, as a book about medication management, faith, and community, and how to hold it together as a Christian while living with serious mental illness. In a word, it's about thriving within one's limitations. We all have them.

Rachel Naomi Remen is one of my greatest teachers. She writes somewhere (I do not recall where) that life, once one encounters chronic illness, becomes a call to a spiritual path. I do not think she means religion here. Rather, the fact is that meeting the needs of an illness bravely can add deep riches to an otherwise barren life. I am on medication and have largely recovered from mental illness symptoms. In order for this to have happened, I had to change my life for the better by learning to do what feeds my soul and not merely my pockets.

It is well-documented that purpose enhances our quality of life when we live with health concerns, especially chronic ones. Having been so open for over ten years now, I have discovered that many have gone through what I and my family have experienced during my illness. When I share about my hospitalizations people feel safe to tell me their stories. And then they swear me to secrecy, and their burdens are lightened by their sharing and I am empowered to continue sharing. This is wonderful, of course, but it also means that there are no bread crumbs for the others who are ill and newly diagnosed to follow into wellness, contributions to family and community, and meaningful friendships and relationships that are not only based on being a care-receiver but that are also able to allow for giving back from time to time, if not always.

Our society sees mental illness only in the mentally ill who are untreated or medicine-resistant because people like me who have found wellness don't often share where they are, where they have been, and that there is hope and a meaning-rich future. Therefore, I have decided to share here with my readers how I came to live well despite serious psychological anguish and the interpersonal drama that still, on occasion, fills my life.

God grabbed me. God's Spirit took me up and set me down in the middle of an open plain strewn with bones. He led me around and among them—a lot of bones! There were bones all over the plain—dry bones, bleached by the sun.

Part I: Disintegration

He said to me, "Son of man, can these bones live?"
I said, "Master God, only you know that."
He said to me, "Prophesy over these bones: 'Dry bones,
listen to the Message of God!'"

God, the Master, told the dry bones, "Watch this: I'm
bringing the breath of life to you and you'll come to life. I'll
attach sinews to you, put meat on your bones, cover you
with skin, and breathe life into you. You'll come alive and
you'll realize that I am God!"

I prophesied just as I'd been commanded. As I prophe-
sied, there was a sound and, oh, rustling! The bones moved
and came together, bone to bone. I kept watching. Sinews
formed, then muscles on the bones, then skin stretched
over them. But they had no breath in them.

He said to me, "Prophesy to the breath. Prophesy, son
of man. Tell the breath, 'God, the Master, says, Come from
the four winds. Come, breath. Breathe on these slain bod-
ies. Breathe life!'"

So I prophesied, just as he commanded me. The breath
entered them and they came alive! They stood up on their
feet, a huge army.

—Ezek 37:1–10

2

Childhood and Early Adulthood

O LORD, support us all the day long,
until the shadows lengthen, and the evening comes,
And the busy world is hushed,
and the fever of life is over, and our work is done.
Then in your mercy, grant us a safe lodging,
and a holy rest, and peace at the last.

—THE BOOK OF COMMON PRAYER

I WAS A DRAMATIC child, difficult, compassionate yet sometimes sneaky, thoughtful but unable to follow through on my thoughtfulness with an even mood. I lacked consistency both as a recipient and as a giver of attention. I lacked consistency.

As I got older, I became intrinsically kinder, someone who would drop everything to help a person in need, but I also kept my rebellious side. Dad tried his best to handle my provocations, but I often escalated the situation by throwing a shoe at him or swearing, even in elementary school. I would not be tamed, though I remember wanting to be. I wanted to feel loved and no love was enough to quench my thirst for attention. Sometimes this is still the case.

Mother was loving, conscious in her raising of her children, and nurturing as could be. She was a stay-at-home mom and taught us to paint in the backyard. I had soccer practice, piano lessons, softball for a while, swim team . . . Mom took me to all of it and encouraged me in everything. And yet, pictures of my childhood suggest that she was unhappy. Dad worked a lot. My brother was my brother—I didn't pay him much mind since he was younger, and we had a good sibling rivalry.

My father and I ruled the house with our moods, spite, and fights. My high school years my parents took my door off its hinges so I couldn't hide when I was running from Dad, and so I lived in a panopticon as an adolescent. I read a great deal.

Early elementary was full of the usual tribulations with being bullied, harassed, and picked on, but it wasn't overly difficult. It just felt like it was difficult for me. My fifth-grade teacher said she had never seen a child as sensitive as I was. When people picked on me it really stayed with me. My sixth-grade year I spent away from my Sacramento home and father and excelled as a soccer player and young pianist during my time living with my grandparents and mother and brother in Fort Worth. We returned to Sacramento the following year and I realized that I had lost all my friends, who had moved on with their lives during my year away. But I was okay.

In high school, I played piano and sang in the church youth band every Sunday, went on mission trips, was offended when friends swore, and was extremely moralistic in everything. I spent lunch in my physics teacher's classroom and read and talked to him about life. Male teachers had the biggest influence on me because I was desperate for a positive father figure since my father worked for much of my childhood and when we were together our way of bonding was difficult for both of us.

I suffered from back aches and body aches in high school as my parents began a four-year process of divorcing. I told my parents I wanted to die when I was thirteen years old. I wouldn't get out of bed and insisted on keeping the room dark. This prompted a trip to the doctor, where I was diagnosed with advanced fibromyalgia and depression. I was put on a high dose of an antidepressant and I began to love life again.

At fifteen I decided to live with my mother.

I often skipped class to read. Never did any drugs. Nor did I drink. Not even a drop until I turned twenty-one. Senior year came around and I realized that I had slacked off grade-wise even though I had studied prodigiously. The trouble was that I hadn't studied what had been assigned. I went to Sonoma State since I didn't get accepted at any of the schools in the University of California system.

At Sonoma State University, I was a piano major and liberal studies major, the latter of which was challenging because I was raised in a Republican household. I fought hard on every lesson, and eventually, came around to my professors' more progressive perspective. This was particularly the case in world religions, where we went to a local Zen monastery, and visited a mosque, among other coursework in Wicca and mysticism. I don't think we focused on Christianity except for reading *The Red Tent*. This was quite a change from the church youth group that I had been attending in high school, which was more than a bit conservative.

I was a major flirt. I wore short skirts and tops with plenty of cleavage paired with push up bras from Victoria's Secret. I was in a long-term, long-distance relationship from high school (with my now husband, Todd) and wasn't promiscuous—didn't even sleep with my boyfriend of many years—but I enjoyed the attention that my body and vivacious attitude afforded me. I had an enthusiastic sense of humor and really blossomed away from home.

I transferred to UC Berkeley for the last two years of under-graduate, having done an independent study in Russian literature with a professor at Sonoma State and fallen in love with it. At Berke-ley, I took twenty-one units a semester, learned to speak Russian flu-ently during those two years, and studied the language four hours a day as a replacement for my piano studies that had sustained me in childhood and while a young college student.

Knowing what I know now, I wonder if this substituting of musical pursuits, which can be quite healing and restorative for the mind, had anything to do with the subsequent onset of the illness given that I replaced music with obsessive study and very few friends. Or was the pull away from friends and toward study a sign of the illness? Regardless, looking back, I see now that what I was experiencing while at Berkeley is typical of people who suffer later from manic depression, also referred to as bipolar disorder. I maintained straight As, graduated summa cum laude, and received, after only two years of study at Berkeley, the departmental citation for excellence in undergraduate research from the Slavic Languages and Literatures Department. I learned French. I reflect on this not with pride, but just shock that I was so obsessed with school.

My honors thesis predicted the end of my twenties, and the irony is not lost on me even now. It was on scandal in Dostoevsky and how scandal scenes, which frequently punctuate Dostoevsky's novels and short stories, anticipate the philosophical thrust of his works. The title was "Scandal: Dostoevsky's Theater of Ideas"; it focused on a close reading of the short story "A Nasty Anecdote" and the book *The Idiot*, the latter of which has always been my favorite work by Dostoevsky. The book ends with the main character Prince Myshkin going insane and spending the rest of his days in a sanatorium, a fancy old-fashioned word for an insane asylum.

Until I found myself in the hospital several years later, I never thought that insanity was real except for the homeless people on the street, and for some reason—God forgive me for even writing this, and know that I no longer feel this way—it seemed as though they had done something to deserve it. Their desperate situation, while pity-inducing, seemed too distant to really reflect on as something that I too was capable of experiencing. I thought insanity was something that was a nice ending to a book—many books end with the main character going insane or killing themselves and I thought this was just for the drama and not the stuff of real life. Usually, they killed themselves as a result of something that they had done wrong, and so it still seemed, though not well-deserved—I would never have said that—it seemed like a logical outcome. The book's narrative demanded that insanity be the logical product of something. This is because humans are meaning-makers. The meaninglessness of suicide is too much of a reality for fiction.[1]

While I was still a student at Berkeley, Todd proposed to me during a camping trip in Yosemite National Park. We were both

---

1. Call, text, or chat 988 Suicide and Crisis Lifeline if you are experiencing thoughts of suicide. They really helped me and are available 24-7. You matter. Do not kill yourself.

overjoyed. I got my teaching credential to be a certified teacher in high schools as an English teacher, and while studying for my teaching certificate I also took graduate classes in literature and eventually entered a PhD program in comparative literature.

What I'm trying to do here is get you to relax, not be so preoccupied with getting so you can respond to God's giving. People who don't know God and the way he works fuss over these things, but you know both God and how he works. Steep yourself in God-reality, God-initiative, God-provisions. You'll find all your everyday human concerns will be met. Don't be afraid of missing out. You're my dearest friends! The Father wants to give you the very kingdom itself.

—Luke 12:29-32

3

How I Lost My Mind

O God our heavenly Father,
you have blessed us and given us dominion over all the earth:
Increase our reverence before the mystery of life;
and give us new insight into your
Purposes for the human race,
and new wisdom and determination in making provision
For its future in accordance with your will;
Through Jesus Christ our LORD. *Amen.*

—*THE BOOK OF COMMON PRAYER*

MAYBE IT WAS MY upbringing, maybe it was medical birth trauma, maybe it was sexual ambiguity in graduate school (see chapter 4), and maybe it was genes since mental illness runs in both lines of my family, but regardless, I slipped into illness over the course of a decade, and life became unbearable when I was twenty-eight. Our current way of framing mental illness, when viewed from a medical perspective, doesn't allow interaction with theology. For a highly academic study of this, I recommend Peter J. Bellini's *The Cerulean Soul*, which is a theology of depression that sets up a way for theology and psychology to interact productively. This allows for a more holistic and integrative pathway to managing mental health and interpersonal challenges. It is not all about meds and boundaries. Yes, meds and boundaries are important, but so is God, and a lot of practitioners aren't trained to think theologically and in an integrative fashion about mental health challenges, social justice issues, and public health. My book *Emergent Grace* wouldn't have even happened without my study of his other book, also fabulous and weighty, *Truth Therapy*.

For the first few years being ill I thought often about the past. The thing I regretted the most was not noticing. Failing to notice and act on the fact that things around me had acquired a deeper poignancy, what my doctor would call salience, than was possible for them in real life. Everything was pregnant with meaning. Light was more golden coming through trees. Music as if merged with my mind, gaining a richness I had never thought possible. It was as though I could feel the granules of the breeze as it brushed across my face, each air molecule individually.

In 2010, graduate school was going great. It seemed I was built for literary analysis, reading into everything and exploring everything in great detail, regularly getting A-pluses on essays. I don't share this to brag but rather to illustrate the nature of my mental condition. I analyze a lot, and do it well, unless I'm having an episode. I was considered brilliant by professors. I started finding it hard to focus and became a little paranoid under stress, but managed to avoid stress by continuing to be a perfectionist. Frankly, everyone is paranoid in graduate school in the secular humanities. You get paid to think and so it's not the free flow of ideas you would expect.

Whatever was normal regarding paranoia under stress, my condition seemed to magnify it. I kept busy and isolated, though I would not have described myself in those terms at the time. It's funny. You read those descriptions of people like me who suffer from disorders such as mine in the DSM (psychiatry's diagnostic manual) and you forget that we are *people* and not our disorder. There is no greater evidence of the soul than the fact that people who are mentally at risk are often acutely distressed by the fact that their brain is distressed.

Interestingly, when I was at my lowest point of the illness, I thought that I was well and everyone else was sick. This trend started early as I started to think that I was dedicated and that everyone else was lazy, even my esteemed professors. I wasn't off-balance, I told myself . . . I was just focused, motivated, and competitive, like any graduate student in her twenties. I taught the first two years of Russian, the first year of German, and was offered a position teaching French, which I declined. I received great reviews and bonded with my students. I really took pride in guiding them through their undergraduate experience.

In 2010, I was accepted into the Fulbright Program to study Russian at Moscow State University and so I lived on campus there over the summer, which my husband fully supported. I got the flu and was unable to leave the dorm room for a week, but then I adjusted to the time change and diet and did well, studying six hours a day and seeing the sights from time to time. I grew and matured on this trip. On the plane on the way back from Russia I reflected on my life in a way that I hadn't been able to before the experience of living abroad and determined that I needed to change for the sake of my marriage, which had definitely taken a back seat to my studies. I realized that my whole life, books had been a coping mechanism and that I needed to be less angry and impatient, less judgmental, more loving; I needed to be intentional about actually thinking about my husband's perspective and considering our life together and not just my own ambition to be a professor. He'd done all the paperwork for me to be able to do the Fulbright. I could write well and be creative, so I wrote the essay in Russian myself. Intellect wasn't the problem. Executive functioning was the problem. I didn't see it that way though. I thought of myself as lazy and berated myself for being a horrible wife, and, on a deeper level, for being so self-absorbed. (Thankfully, since then, I have become an attentive wife; plus, the self-hatred that would lead me to call myself a "horrible wife" and "self-absorbed" has lessened over time.)

"If I don't change, I wouldn't give our marriage more than ten years," I wrote. That was probably true. Something needed to change. And it did, but it wasn't pretty for the next several years.

They say that crazy people are scary. That there is a certain absence in our gaze that is difficult to put one's finger on. But has the crazy person lost her soul? What has happened to the soul of the man who has gone insane? Is he still there? The answer, quite simply, is yes. These are still people. People who are being overtaken by an illness just as a seizure will seize its sufferer. We are still people. I was a person. And I still am.

And I was a person who then began to really struggle. Little things, like the inability to concentrate, began to affect me more and more, but I did not have insight into what was happening to me because I had received no mental health education, aside from through scholarly books on classic literature that featured mental illness prominently. That, and also antiquated articles by Freud from the early 1900s (let's just say mental health theories and treatments have come a long way, thankfully, since then).

I was reading works of literature from the seventeenth through the early twentieth centuries in five different languages, writing papers about them, and getting great grades. But what I wouldn't tell anyone: I spent all of my time on the papers and couldn't concentrate as a student enough to read the works unless I was writing on them. I couldn't manage a planner; I couldn't keep my office clean . . . This was definitely different from my undergraduate and first graduate years.

My adviser said that I didn't trust the faculty. Another professor noted that I was the only student who seemed to hop back and forth between advisers, unable to commit. What I would later find out, many years later, is that this is common to people who struggle with paranoia, plus I also had legitimate interpersonal stressors (see chapter 4). The hierarchical positioning required for most positions as a student, especially as a graduate student, is deeply triggering and the only way to alleviate the paranoia is to step outside of the social structure. To change advisors, to not follow the syllabus which feels like a method of control . . . I struggle with this to this day, though to a much lesser extent now that I'm on the right diet and medicine, as I earn a Master of Divinity (a religious degree) in an online school. I think that the school is online is what makes it possible for me to thrive in it. When I have difficulties, I focus on my life at home and my friendships and family. But at this earlier period, I had abandoned my family emotionally in favor of work and my friends and mentors were all based in my graduate program. I had put all my eggs in one basket, and it was an idolatrous one.

I was triggered by the thought of restricting my focus and so I applied and was welcomed into the German department as well as the comparative literature department and therefore I was working toward an MA in German as I did my PhD coursework in comparative literature. I also took courses in linguistics and regularly received an A-plus in those. Again, I don't share to brag. I'm just describing what happened, particularly since there is bias against those of us with serious mental health challenges, that we are unintelligent.

It was a linguistics professor who later commented on how many plates I had spinning: "Erin, eventually you will have to focus." She seemed off base at the time—I had thought my diversity of interests simply made me special, unique. It does make me special and unique, but it also leads to a scattered consciousness.

I had been reading Dostoevsky and Kafka, writing successfully on works like *Stationmaster Thiel*. These works can be very disturbing, and I had been reading them for over a decade. This is what I lived on in high school. Over a short time, however, I became exceedingly sensitive to scenes of violence or rape. When I read them, it felt like it was happening to me when I read it. It began making me ill. I absorbed literature and it was as though the barrier between text and reality was ruptured.

It wasn't traumatic however until I was assigned a film. When a professor assigned a film to me that was off the syllabus supposedly due to my interest in Soviet film, *The Rabbit Is Me*—about a woman who is in a sustained relationship with a professorial lawyer who takes advantage of the power dynamic to exploit her sexually—I began to disintegrate. It is a Cold War–era film, the woman wants to study Russian and become a translator, and she is destroyed over the course of their sexually abusive relationship. When I watched it, something inside of me broke. I became obsessed with the idea that it had been assigned because the professor wanted to traumatize me. I wrote to him, telling him that one of my worries being in graduate school was the fear of being institutionalized, and not only metaphorically because of the potential indoctrination involved as one pursues a graduate education. No, I wrote, I was worried about being institutionalized in both senses of the word. Worried about being literally put in an institution. A mental institution. I had never thought I would end up in one, they had only been a figment of the literary imagination the day before, and yet suddenly it seemed inevitable. After the film, it was as if I had begun to leak. That the real and the symbolic worlds had merged, and I had been sutured into the film.

He pushed me hard to do a presentation on the film to the class even though I was auditing. I confided in him that I had been abused as a child and needed grace and couldn't do the assignment. I'd never used my personal life as an excuse—though now I frequently do just that so that people can manage their expectations of me—but I didn't have words for how inappropriate the assignment had been, especially since I was auditing. Why would I have to present on it? Why was he repeatedly insisting on it? He oversaw my TA-ship, and I wanted to teach for his department the next year, so I stuffed my profound alarm and brushed it aside. Or so I thought.

The professor apologized and pleaded ignorance of the trauma and violation that I had experienced when he assigned, and insisted that I present on the film. Maybe it was accidental, though in my heart of hearts, acknowledging I may be wrong, I doubt it very much. He was frequently checking me out and I was flirting with him and even wrote a provocative paper on the poems of adultery by the Russian rakish poet Tiutchev in a previous quarter while in his class. Life seemed to move on. I stopped going to his class, alerted to the possibility that there was a cruelty under his flirtations and that he might be more serious in his interests, and that they could be more sinister.

Do you want to be counted wise, to build a reputation for wisdom? Here's what you do: Live well, live wisely, live humbly. It's the way you live, not the way you talk, that counts. Mean-spirited ambition isn't wisdom. Boasting

that you are wise isn't wisdom. Twisting the truth to make yourselves sound wise isn't wisdom. It's the furthest thing from wisdom—it's animal cunning, devilish plotting. Whenever you're trying to look better than others or get the better of others, things fall apart and everyone ends up at the others' throats.

—Jas 3:13–16

4

What Ultimately Happened

Almighty and most merciful God,
we remember before you all poor and neglected persons
Whom it would be easy for us to forget:
the homeless and the destitute, the old and the sick,
And all who have none to care for them.
Help us to heal those who are broken in body or spirit,
And to turn their sorrow into joy.
Grant this, Father, for the love of your Son,
who for our sake became poor, Jesus Christ our LORD. *Amen.*

—THE BOOK OF COMMON PRAYER

AGAIN, I WAS STUDYING adultery in literature, and now film, and eventually it caught up with me in my own personal life in graduate school with the professor I was studying it with, the one who had assigned the film. Stricken by attacks of conscience, I prostrated myself before God one afternoon after lunch. I was living in Heidelberg. It was a frantic moment. At this time, I was away from my family for the sake of my "career advancement," or whatever you might call that perilous journey, a pilgrimage, toward the ivory tower I had enthusiastically embarked upon. I never prayed anymore. Instead, I worked, studying philosophy, the atheist Nietzsche, where only years before I had studied my Bible. I never thought about God. Nor did I go to church. I even smirked when they passed the collection plate on the rare occasions I attended. But this day, I prayed deeply. I prayed to God that he would reshape my life. "I don't want to be like this!" I whispered on my knees.

I was ashamed of myself, of my thoughts, and of my ambition, and I judged accurately that I was impure in my motivations and in my heart because, though it shames me now to say it, and though I love my husband very much, I was interested in that man and we had grown close after I had shared that the film had traumatized me. He had taken me under his wing. My first therapist, a brilliant man, who helped me unravel what had happened, called it trauma bonding. He explained that when we are bound traumatically to our parents as children, it becomes easier to form similarly unhealthy and unhelpful bonds in future relationships. All it takes is a trauma and then we latch on to the negative core radiating from that initial painful interaction.

Sensing in my soul what I could not tell myself directly, I begged Jesus to draw me out of myself and the world that I had both created around myself and been born into, and to show me the way home. Whither I knew not. But I begged that day to be purified in my heart.

There is a providence that watches over each person's life as they navigate its waters and it supplies two guides, one that calls one forward, and the other that calls one back. Kierkegaard, in describing this, explains that these guides are not in opposition to each other, however. "Nor," he continues, "do they leave the wanderer standing there in doubt, confused by the double call. Rather the two are in eternal understanding with each other. For the one beckons forward to the Good, the other calls man back from evil."

Whatever your own religious beliefs, know that I'm not one to pressure others. All I can speak to is that I feel Jesus in my heart. Jesus or no, it is common knowledge that people who suffer with mood disorders coupled with "daddy issues" are more prone than many to be carried away by their passions into affairs. And Christian though I was, happily married to my high school sweetheart though I was, it almost went this way with me, too. I wanted the good as a Christian, yet I craved the bad.

I can remember the day that I faked my research interest in film so that it more closely resonated with the research interests with this older professor who was very like my father in looks and also in atmosphere. I went to his office hours and made sure that I fastened my cross onto my neck before going. I knew it was wrong—hence the cross—but the repetition compulsion, whereby we reenact our childhood traumas unconsciously, is not to be tampered with in one's mid-twenties. It is just a matter of having been set up to self-destruct as a child.

Jesus says to do good deeds with one hand and not to tell the other hand what the first hand is doing. I tried a similar stunt, but substituting the good with the evil, flirting with desire while telling myself that all was well and playing the part of a good wife. A large part of it was unconscious, and yet at the same time, deep down, I knew what was happening. Thinking back now on my life at that time, it all has a surreal quality.

At the end of the day, I did need two calls, one away from evil and one toward the Good.

And so, I prayed to be purified. I am now pure, and yet, initially, my heart was not purified; nor was I delivered from my symptoms. I did what I could, ripping myself from the academia context with nothing to replace it with. I changed advisers and told the chair what had been going on with this professor, and that he had wanted me to fly out to Berlin with him, and she reported it. It was before #MeToo and so my own reputation was what ended up tarnished amongst the professors and graduate students, who heard about it. I was dropped and ghosted by my dissertation chair.

"I just need to finish my MA—no need for a PhD!" I told myself. I reminded myself that I had always wanted to be a writer in the first place, and not of academic works, but my heart would sink every time I remembered the straight As on my transcripts since the beginning of my higher education career. Grades had assuredly become an idol, but they also were a sign of dedication. I was deeply dedicated to learning and growing, though I had stunted my personal development in favor of book learning and transactional learning (in other words, grades).

Back into the mess I went the following year to finish my MA. What I see now in looking back was that I was starting to suffer seriously from mental illness. Day-to-day activities common to being a graduate student, such as going to office hours, teaching, grading papers, and writing them, were starting to become literally impossible. I still remember getting a D on an assignment, utterly panicking and asking for a redo, and then getting an A-plus after the episode passed. I had tried my best and gotten a D. That had never in my entire life happened. It was confusing because I looked fine, though I was starting to lose weight, eat less, and drink less water. I drank a lot of coffee and ate unhealthy food because that's what I had always done. I didn't realize that what you eat and drink matters for mental health.

I was occasionally pacing around my office, and often sharing paranoid thoughts with friends, thinly veiled of course so that no one could connect the dots and know specifically what was going on. What I know now is that the vagueness of paranoia is what fuels it. So, really, I didn't know what was going on but, meanwhile, I was very worried about "it"—whatever "it" was. I wouldn't have been able to tell you myself. I would talk in Russian with friends on the phone so that I wouldn't be "reported" to the crisis team that the university had started after I confided in the chair that I had been dissociative and was having a hard time. After the crisis team had happened, doors kept shutting for me. I was no longer a potential future colleague to professors. No, I was a troubled student.

I already shared some of my struggles and that they were due to mental illness, but there was also a more normal, human dimension to my existence. I could only wonder now: what was all this learning *for*? Only in the abstract were the books I read related to people. What was all this learning *for*? I had lived and breathed literature, putting myself in the position of the protagonists for over a decade, and it was suddenly like, for the first time I realized that *I*, even *I*, was a person.

I confided in my linguistics professor, who replied after sharing that she had also been courted by an older professor as a graduate student, that, "The academy is a business, and it behooves you to take all emotion out of it. It is exclusively for honing the intellect." Such revelations are part of the coming-of-age story of all ambitious twenty-somethings. But it was paired with moods that made what would be normal human experiences and thoughts, unbearable and obsessive.

I left my PhD program even though I had already done all of the coursework for a PhD and had straight As and had been a Fulbright scholar and summa cum laude at Cal. There was not only a deep loss but also a feeling of relief and escape and of having chosen rightly to protect my marriage from careerism and leering older men.

I felt this love for academia after I abandoned it. But I also thought that leaving it would free me from ambition, pride, and careerism. This was premature. I had struggled with learning for the sake of learning for all of my life and didn't understand it was something to be struggled against. Now that the suffering was hard upon me something else replaced my thoughts of books and that professor who had been pursuing me. Thoughts of suicide.[1]

Once off balance, it is hard to recover.

As soon as I started having suicidal thoughts, I got a psychiatrist at once because I had been a TA in a class on fantasy and the supernatural that talked about serious mental illness and how a lot of writers of fantastic and supernatural literature live with mental health conditions and that many die by suicide. My background in undergraduate and graduate school was psychology and psychoanalysis in *literature*. All of a sudden my temptation- and suicide-filled literary world was becoming my own lived reality. I could no longer read fiction. I still usually can't. Oh, the hubris of thinking you could study it, such a profoundly human medium, as though you yourself weren't human, without getting burned!

I had removed myself from an environment of temptation, renewed a commitment to my faith, had not forsaken my marriage or betrayed my vows, and was granted a job teaching French and

---

1. Call, text, or chat 988 Suicide and Crisis Lifeline if you are experiencing thoughts of suicide. They really helped me and are available 24-7. You matter. Do not kill yourself.

Spanish full time at a wonderful high school. Everything from the outside looked wonderful. I was finishing two MAs, which I would finish in the next few years, and had learned that getting a tenure track job in the humanities is akin to winning a lottery, so I didn't even have sour grapes. Or at least not too bad. Though I was wildly jealous of a friend who had secured a post-doctoral fellowship at a prestigious university.

Every day I thought of driving my car off the road.

I would call my doctor. He would tell me I was manic, ask me if I had slept, and increase my medicine. I didn't realize that increasing antipsychotics, which diminished my vivaciousness in the classroom as well as out, also lead to significant weight gain, particularly if you don't change the way you eat.

My students started asking if I was pregnant. To this day I sometimes get asked. This is hurtful, but I no longer identify with my looks to the extent I did in my twenties, when this was going on. So, at the time, the weight gain was devastating. I had not understood the extent to which heaviness is equated with moral failure in our culture. As a result of the antipsychotic medication, I also stopped having my period (another side effect). I haven't had a period in eight years.

All the while I kept teaching—well, it became less and less like real teaching as the months, and then the years, wore on. Todd would write me love notes of encouragement and talk to me through my lunch breaks as I shared my concern that my phone was bugged.

We often hear stories of happy people who are loved by everyone and always so positive that commit suicide.[2] It is so easy to seem pulled together when you are crumbling from within. From my yearbook my first year of teaching high school:

"Dear Madame Grimm, I will miss French class over the summer and will try to keep my French up and I hope I will see you next year in French 3! Thank you for making me more confident in French

---

2. You matter. Do not kill yourself.

and giving me a passion for the language. I have learned a lot this year. THANK YOU!"

"Dear Mme Grimm, you are my absolute favorite teacher! (Don't tell the others.) You are so light-hearted and positive and you brighten my day—EVERY SINGLE DAY! Best teacher ever!"

"Hey Mme Grimm, I hope you enjoy the brownies and have a great summer. Over the summer I am taking a Latin class at Sac State. Thank you for getting me interested in foreign languages. You are and always will be my favorite foreign language teacher!"

When I received these messages from students, I wasn't even proud. Such entries are the fruit of good teaching paired with strong teacher-student relationships. When I rediscovered the yearbook a year after having been hospitalized, however, it seemed unfathomable that at any time in my life I would have been such a good teacher with such good, positive relationships with students. My self-concept as a professional had been that damaged. It has been recovered since, but it's humbler. That's probably for the best.

You're blessed when you stay on course,
walking steadily on the road revealed by God.
You're blessed when you follow his directions,
doing your best to find him.
That's right—you don't go off on your own;
you walk straight along the road he set.
You, God, prescribed the right way to live;
now you expect us to live it.
Oh, that my steps might be steady,
keeping to the course you set;
Then I'd never have any regrets
in comparing my life with your counsel.
I thank you for speaking straight from your heart;
I learn the pattern of your righteous ways.
I'm going to do what you tell me to do;
don't ever walk off and leave me.

—Ps 119:1–8

5

The Break

O Almighty God,
who pours out on all who desire it the spirit of grace and supplication:
Deliver us, when we draw near to you,
from coldness of heart and wanderings of mind,
that with steadfast thoughts and kindled affections
we may worship you in spirit and in truth;
through Jesus Christ our LORD. Amen.

—THE BOOK OF COMMON PRAYER

THE MEDICATION WORKED. AND SO, I went off of it a year later, keeping on the mood-stabilizer but with no antipsychotic because I didn't want to be overweight. Mood stabilizers alone are a typical treatment for many people who struggle with bipolar disorder, which is what the doctor thought I had. Old habits resumed themselves and I began calling Todd again throughout the day with my worries and paranoia. I went to a health cleanse over the winter break, my stress was so great. My world was closing in on me. Everyone was against me. The detox—I've never done drugs, it was just a health cleanse—had cost two thousand dollars and my mom had gladly paid for it, though my doctor recommended against it because it would clear me of all my medications.

"Oh well," I had said, "It will only be for a week."

Over that vacation, the paranoia increased and finally, urged by a colleague upon return to the school, I went to the emergency room. The attending physician recommended an antidepressant, diagnosing me with anxiety and complex PTSD. Because my paranoia and the oncoming delusions were not bizarre, and because I was outraged that I had gained fifty pounds the last time I was on an antipsychotic, they did not put me on an antipsychotic. I objected, vehemently refused antipsychotics, and thought that they were poison for your brain and to be avoided at all costs.

The doctor explained to Todd, "She says she was raped."

"Since watching a film in graduate school triggered her," Todd explained, "she has discovered that she must have been sexually abused as a child. This week, her body therapist said that she knew she had been raped as a child. Now memories are coming to her of these events. Starting this week."

The doctor continued. "Her mind is racing, give it a couple of months and she will need antipsychotics, unless we can interrupt the anxiety and give her mind a break with an antidepressant." She put me on 50 milligrams of an antidepressant, which was a low dose.

I dutifully went into the office of my school the next day and put the antidepressant on my list of medications that I was on, relieved that this doctor did not think, as my other doctors had, that I was bipolar. And with that she won me over unconditionally. Plus, she had an amazing bedside manner.

It was incredible the change in self-image I experienced being relieved of the label "bipolar." I started drafting a book about how a complex PTSD diagnosis saved my life and rid me of my symptoms, thanks to the right treatment, an antidepressant. I wrote that I was almost written off as mentally ill, had almost lost all of my sense of self-worth, crippled by a stigmatizing diagnosis, but I had been redeemed by a change in diagnosis that had made life wonderful.

"You should try it too!" I probably wrote at some point.

This is how profound the effects of labels can be. I didn't care about how I was reacting to the medicine, I cared that I had been declared normal and spared the label that other doctors on their pedestal had slapped on me. The healing balm of being put in the "normal category"—PTSD is a normal, natural response to something traumatic—erased any sense of alarm that my regular doctor had imparted on me before I had gone on the health cleanse. The idea that being off a mood stabilizer for a week was causing a psychotic break could not have been further from my mind. The fact that antidepressants amplify psychosis in some cases didn't matter because at that point, though it had been several years of symptoms with an eye of the storm in between (thanks to the antipsychotic), no one had told me I was experiencing psychosis. If they had known in the first place. I certainly hadn't known it. I didn't even know what "psychosis" really was except that if you were psychotic, it meant that you were irredeemable, lost and dead to the world, and probably going to kill someone. Obviously, I no longer think this way. I am vehemently opposed to such a worldview, and I myself have never been a threat to others, but that was just my basic understanding as a layperson who had unconsciously judged people experiencing serious mental health problems. We must change the story of how people who are struggling are characterized in our society. Knowing that psychosis is a medical condition would have been much healthier and led to immediate relief as I came to terms with the weight gain in favor of a normal life. But this isn't what happened. The psychosis grew, paired with mania. Mania is quite pleasurable before the crash.

I had never felt better. I could focus and see things differently now. Planning problems and confusion were gone. I was happy again. I had been on an antidepressant as a teenager without any antipsychotic or mood stabilizer, so why did I need them now? I wasn't bipolar, I was told (now I know I have schizoaffective disorder, which is a combination of schizophrenia and bipolar disorder).

I switched doctors to the emergency room doctor to liberate myself from the oppressive old school doctor who objectified me by putting a label on me and wouldn't increase my antidepressant or take me off the mood stabilizer. My new doctor did both. She bumped me up to 200 milligrams of the antidepressant, which is often considered the largest dose, and she took me off the mood stabilizer.

"Don't do it," the other doctor had said.

I did it.

We started slowly. I started up at 50 milligrams of the anti-depressant. The next day I went to a friend's house convinced that his daughter was going to kill herself,[1] to "rescue" her on God's advice—though there was no evidence of this suicidal ideation or intention. My friend spent an hour talking me out of my thinking as I sat on the porch with his other daughter watching me as I talked on her cell phone because I had raced out without mine to go and "save a life." I still have a direct reaction to antidepressants. They always trigger psychotic thinking. I am on antidepressants to this day, but on a very high dose of an antipsychotic to counteract this trend.

"Wow, if this happens again, let me know," I said to him. "Because this is crazy. I've never had this happen before . . ."

I started having flashbacks of rape that were eerily like the scenes of sexual exploitation in that film, *The Rabbit Is Me*, that had been assigned. I couldn't have sex with my husband; I would shriek out that I was being raped. The word "rape" sent me over the edge. Words and memories my body therapist reconstructed, and symbols from fiction and TV fused when I went to a new therapist, one who did EMDR. EMDR had worked great for me *before* psychosis. I told her what my body therapist had told me and shared my memories of rape with her. We worked through the images, and it was as if my mind was being steadily compressed in a vice with every twist and turn of the conversation. It was only when I left the office, however, that my mind was as if shattered.

Clinically, a person who is psychotic cannot assess to see if what is being said, thought, or felt is real or not. This is called reality testing. Everything that that therapist said she knew had happened to me really became for me as if it had happened. She touched me sexually and said she knew I had been raped. I actually did suffer from complex PTSD, but not to these proportions. It became debilitating.

Pacing, mind racing, and then being broken open . . . and shattered. Three months later I almost died, running into a hospital emergency room unadmitted asking the doctors to stab me to

1. Call, text, or chat 988 Suicide and Crisis Lifeline if you are experiencing thoughts of suicide. They really helped me and are available 24-7. You matter. Do not kill yourself.

death and shrieking, before falling over, "Everyone knows I've been raped," because I was experiencing delusions that block the boundary between self and world, which erase the ego boundary. So that what I was thinking, I felt everyone else was also thinking, and that everyone knew everything about me.

I was involuntarily committed, and left the hospital two weeks later, still trapped in the delusion that my psychiatrist at the hospital said I may always, for the rest of my life, believe was true: that the whole Sacramento valley had thought that I was going to sue them and take over the county and that they thought that I would destroy the careers, livelihoods, and joy of all the residents of Sacramento. I shared my desire to clear my name to the doctor:

"Please tell everyone that I'm not going to sue them." This was probably lingering terror from graduate school, when the school anticipated that I would sue them. The small coterie of professors in my departments in graduate school, and my fellow graduate students, had been magnified in my mind to astounding proportions as I imagined the whole county fearing I would pursue them legally.

My psychiatrist wrote on the pad he carried with him, "Lacks insight." This is a formal term (the real term is anosognosia) meaning that a person doesn't know that they are sick.

If you have ever seen people who resist medications, it is often because they have lost track of the fact that they are suffering from mental health symptoms. If they ever sensed that they had begun to slip in the first place. Psychosis often sneaks up on you gradually, over the course of years, and after time the illness becomes normalized. Without my husband I would have become homeless. My psychosis story is successful, at least so far, because I am committed to medicine, and medicine allows me to be in community. Because of community, because of the support of family and friends, I do well. But it also makes it that much harder when there are interpersonal challenges within that community. It is very easy for relationships with professors in particular to sour with me because I am such an honest and direct person and am an educator by training, and some people don't like to hear the truth, even when it is gently given. (Sometimes what I think is "the truth" is really just my own opinion—a hazard we're all prone to as humans).

When I'm dealing with the fallout from that, I am prone to panic, self-doubt, and suicidal ideation. When that happens, I read the Bible, out loud, for many hours at a time (about which I write more below). I email mentors who love me and who are very emotionally mature, they don't engage with the specifics, and they are supportive. I also have a rule that I don't gossip about or demonize people when sharing with mentors about a person (in 2010–15 I demonized people frequently, though never with mentors because I was a twenty-something-year-old professional still trying to make her way in the world—but regarding demonizing people, medicine helps alleviate that tendency).

I focus on being healthy and well so I don't have to bother Todd about my drama; on rare occasions when it's really bad I tell Todd I'm dealing with suicidal thoughts, and I immediately feel better and he asks me what I need. Usually I just need to sit and watch a simple show like *The Great British Baking Show* or something else totally innocent, mindless, and positive. If it's really bad I call my doctor and do whatever he says, which is usually going up on my antipsychotic a couple of days.

My goal, however, is to practice self-care in the first place and to keep healthy bonds in the community by caring about the perspectives of others more sensitive than myself to criticism. In this way, I stay healthy. I try to stay healthy especially for Todd's sake, so that he can live a calm and happy life. Knowing I'm trying my best to be the best wife possible is very healing to me. Especially after all he's been through. He deserves that.

The doctor said my hospitalization was the result of a profoundly abusive childhood. Everyone, you see, thought I was a rape victim—I don't think I am, but I still, to this day, don't know for sure.

I run to you, God; I run for dear life.
Don't let me down!
Take me seriously this time!
Get down on my level and listen,
and please—no procrastination!
Your granite cave a hiding place,

your high cliff nest a place of safety.

You're my cave to hide in,
my cliff to climb.
Be my safe leader,
be my true mountain guide.
Free me from hidden traps;
I want to hide in you.
I've put my life in your hands.
You won't drop me,
you'll never let me down.

I hate all this silly religion,
but you, God, I trust.
I'm leaping and singing in the circle of your love;
you saw my pain,
you disarmed my tormentors,
You didn't leave me in their clutches
but gave me room to breathe.
Be kind to me, God—
I'm in deep, deep trouble again.
I've cried my eyes out;
I feel hollow inside.
My life leaks away, groan by groan;
my years fade out in sighs.
My troubles have worn me out,
turned my bones to powder.

—Ps 31:1–10

PART II

MindBodySoul

O God, you made us in your own image and redeemed us
Through Jesus your Son:
Look with compassion on the whole human family;
Take away the arrogance and hatred which
Infect our hearts;
Break down the walls that separate us;
Unite us in bonds of love; and work through our struggle and
Confusion to accomplish your purposes on earth; that, in
Your good time, all nations and races may serve you in
Harmony around your heavenly throne;
Through Jesus Christ our LORD. Amen.

—*THE BOOK OF COMMON PRAYER*

MIND

A cluttered mind springs forth from the soul's idolatry.
Communion with God returns unity and balance.
Remember: we strain when we think something up.
But there is no strain when we get something down.

BODY

What would it be like to really feel?
To relax muscles rather than tighten them?
To allow for sorrow to wash over us and to welcome it as it yields a
     calm maturity?
The body and soul must be aligned, submitting to God.
We are not God.
We are not God and God cares for us. Without care God is not love.
God is love, and Christ is LORD: He is within me and he surrounds
     me.
Speak, Christ: in what way are you making your presence known
     to me?
What spiritual gifts have you blessed me with?
In the Book of Common Prayer, it is written,

> *Almighty God, whose loving hand has given us all that we*
> *possess: Grant us grace that we may honor you with our*
> *substance, and, remembering the account which we must*

one day give, may we be faithful stewards of your bounty,
through Jesus Christ our Lord, Amen.

SOUL

Make your words a blessing,
Make your words a delight . . .
About words to God:
Use prayer, meditation, Scripture, and spiritual reading.
Begin with praise.
Words to humans:
Heal with them, choose them with care.
Keep them to a minimum until the Spirit strikes.
Then let them flow.

IT IS ODD THAT so often in writing about hope we forget that to arrive at hope after a life of trauma is a gift of the grace of God alone. My cyclically abusive upbringing was surrounded by the protective love of my mother and even—yes, it is strange and hard to fathom, but undeniably true—the doting love of my father. He really did love me. And I knew this. He still does, and I still love him, though for a while I hated him deeply, blaming him exclusively for my mental illness even though I had brain damage when born and was also sexually harassed. From a psychological perspective this is the craziness of complex PTSD. Namely, that it is repeated trauma that takes place in a loving relationship where you are dependent on the person who terrifies you—here, my father or that professor—and rely on their care (or your TA-ship), and perhaps even return their affections.

People sometimes wonder why people who are pursued by professors or bosses and who don't like it don't complain or leave, but if you're raised in a recurrently abusive environment, the idea that you can just leave doesn't occur to you. A family friend who was a professor at a nearby university was the one who told me that a PhD didn't make you smarter than others, it was just something that some people do sometimes. A PhD means you took coursework and passed exams and wrote a dissertation. Before he said that, it had never occurred to me that I could leave an environment where the professor in charge of my TA-ship assigned me to present things off-syllabus that were sexually explicit while I was auditing (and therefore not responsible for doing any work). Or where my PhD chair had dropped me after I had reported sexual harassment, for that matter.

Don't get me wrong. My fears weren't unwarranted, because you need references to transfer schools or jobs and if you've burned bridges, even if it's by being sexually harassed and someone else has burned your bridge, you're at a dead end. When we report harassment, we lose relationships and allies. This doesn't mean that we shouldn't report necessarily, but it's just naïve to think that reports of harassment always end positively. This isn't legal advice, but what I wish I had done was get a legal consultant for myself outside of the university. The university sexual harassment office is there to prevent lawsuits, not to enforce protections or justice. That's just my experience. Also, it is hilarious that I expected that confidentiality would be maintained. Another thing: always network beyond your immediate bubble. I was met with sympathy and support initially, and then with disbelief, and then with resentment and disbelief, and finally department invitations stopped coming into my email inbox. #MeToo unfolded a few years later and was liberating because it made me realize that it wasn't all in my head. If I had cast a wider net, I would have had more leverage as I left—though that is why tenured professors always go after the younger graduate students, isn't it? We have no leverage.

Judith Butler—who wrote *Trauma and Recovery*, the book which details the diagnosis of complex PTSD—likens abusive upbringings to being a hostage victim. To this day, when I interact with my dad it feels almost as if nothing difficult ever happened between us, though of course this is not entirely true. I often forget that the place where I suffered from sexual harassment was so bad, because I have memories of my beautiful office there, dinner with friends, and all the rest, plus the professor himself was extra kind to me, though this kindness had a darker character to it, marred as it was by his less-than-pure intentions and my own impurity of thought and will.

Indeed, there's this dark underbelly of fear that permeates my memories of my graduate school when I'm not doing well, but on other days, when I look at my resume, I sometimes still feel pride. More often than not, though, it's just a sense of neutrality that pervades me when I think back on successes. This is something I have gradually come to see as a gift, because it has made me see the intrinsic worth and equality of all people. The rich and famous, and the unhoused and mentally ill, we are all equally worthy of love and respect, and the weaker are to be treated with greater care. Indeed, high school diplomas, BAs, MAs, and PhDs are markers of how you've spent your time and indicate that you might have received a certain training here and there, but that's pretty much it. Tell that to a twenty-year-old though, or a eighty-year-old who never encounter job-related trauma, and you'll get a blank stare.

I still see my father a couple of times a year, and though I love seeing him, it still takes me a couple of weeks to come back to myself after seeing him. Somehow, energetically, he seems to sense when I'm doing well and starting to move forward with my life. At such times, he calls and usually comes for a visit, which is all well and good, I guess. We enjoy ourselves for the most part. But it is also a little stressful because he doesn't acknowledge what happened and has never apologized, so that there's this sort of fake veneer to it all. This has been there for as long as I can remember. I sometimes wonder if this isn't where the "schizo"-splitness of my schizoaffective disorder comes from. When I'm around him I experience amnesia about what I've been through with him, and all the integrative work I've done goes out the window. I'm still happy to see him, but it's just very confusing and disruptive to my sense of self and inner narrative. I guess this was always the case and that it will always be the case. He was so affectionate, syrupy sweet even—and yet he also full-body-weighing-on-me pinned me to the ground on one occasion and shrieked at me that he hated me. My ears went numb as though I'd been at the shooting range without earplugs in. Then he drove me to school.

The ebbs and flows of rupture, release, and calm are scarred into my mind even though I lead a peaceful and happy life. It comes out now with my email patterns, and in other ways I'm sure, too. Some of my communications are erratic and confusing. People sometimes write me saying they're not sure how to respond. It's probably just echoes of trauma coming out of my fingertips as they hit the keyboard. There is no possible response that would still me fully. I am restless.

If I were my own friend, I would tell myself that I shouldn't feel pressured to keep him in my life. I know that I don't keep in touch out of guilt, but out of love. He has changed, mellowed, and matured. Our whole family has. I was going to go through all the details of the abuse that I had experienced and even had some great scenes in first drafts of this book, but it's not what I am choosing to focus on, and over time it does indeed become a choice, minus the occasional PTSD flashback (they used to be constant, so I'm acknowledging my privilege that my medicine has diminished my PTSD significantly).

One time Dad said he didn't know that what he had done would have impacted me to the extent that it had. This seems to be the closest that he will ever come to offering an apology. It's probably just lingering terror from when I was very small, but I genuinely feel like it wouldn't be safe to be in the same room with him were he to be alerted to his former abuse and its impact on me. He just does not see himself that way. It's just sort of unfathomable, the thought that I would tell him he devastated me and disrupted the course of my career by giving me bad relating habits to sinister men, and that part of me is still afraid of him. However, I presume one day he will read this book. Who knows?

In many ways he is a great man. Over the years he has become more consistently so.

I entitled this section MindBodySoul all one word because they are, indeed, all interconnected, and I believe that the disunion of these three elements is what leads to all sorts of mayhem in the lives of people suffering from chronic illness, aside from, perhaps, genetic disorders, which are pretty fixed as I understand them as a layperson.

Since my brain struggles regularly, I treat it with medication and vitamins.

For a while, in fact, I called my medication a vitamin, following the promptings of a creative psychiatrist (the one who put me on the high antidepressant and assured me I wasn't bipolar—I try to take something good from everyone). However, I have started calling my medication my "grandmother." I had two great women as grandmothers. Oma died when I was six. The other one's name was Cornelia and she just died in 2019. My mom's mom.

In 2019, the same year she died, Grandma Cornelia looked at me deeply, on a day when I had just gone up on my medicine significantly, and she told me, pointedly, that she thought that I was doing particularly well that day.

"Whatever you're doing today," she said, "keep it up."

It was one of the most profound and impactful moments of my life with her, and it was a parting gift that she would have said such a thing because people of her generation were not always keen to take mental health medication seriously. She said at another time that one of the saddest periods of her life was 2011–16, the years when I was most ill, because she had just lost her husband, my Grandpa George, and she lost me because that was the same year that I began the five-year process of losing my mind (what is known as first-episode psychosis).

Anyone who meets a testing challenge head-on and manages to stick it out is mighty fortunate. For such persons loyally in love with God, the reward is life and more life. Don't let anyone under pressure to give in to evil say, "God is trying to trip me up." God is impervious to evil, and puts evil in no one's way. The temptation to give in to evil comes from us and only us. We have no one to blame but the leering, seducing flare-up of our own lust. Lust gets pregnant, and has a baby: sin! Sin grows up to adulthood, and becomes a real killer. So, my very dear friends, don't get thrown off course. Every desirable and beneficial gift comes out of heaven. The gifts are rivers of light cascading down from the Father of Light. There is nothing deceitful in God, nothing two-faced, nothing fickle. He brought us to life using the true Word, showing us off as the crown of all his creatures.

—Jas 1:12–18

6

Faith Healing

LORD, make us instruments of your peace.
Where there is hatred, let us sow love;
Where there is injury, pardon;
Where there is discord, union;
Where there is doubt, faith;
Where there is despair, hope;
Where there is darkness, light;
Where there is sadness, joy.
Grant that we may not so much
Seek to be consoled as to console;
To be understood as to understand;
To be loved as to love.
For it is in giving that we receive;
It is in pardoning that we are pardoned;
And it is in dying that
We are born to eternal life.

—*THE BOOK OF COMMON PRAYER,*
A Prayer Attributed to Saint Francis

I HAD NEVER BEEN more confused after being hospitalized. I just had no way to frame life. There weren't words. I didn't know what "first-episode psychosis" was at the time, but it is the term that describes the first multiyear descent into the madness that psychosis brings. This term captures well the fact that initially there aren't words in the vocabulary of the sufferer to gain a grasp of what is happening. And no one else knows how to describe the descent into madness unless they are trained. Maybe it's just a bad day? A bad month? A bad year?

A bad five years that land you ultimately in the hospital is what it was for me. It would have lasted much longer if I had not committed to always, always, always taking medication.

Children often don't report abuse because, even if they know it's wrong, they don't have vocabulary to convey what is going on in the first place. If you don't know the words for all the body parts, how are you going to say that you're being touched inappropriately? Mental health education for children and young adults would be an important step for young adults who are starting to live with psychosis to know how to intervene in their own progressive suffering. In absence of this knowledge and vocabulary, I turned to Christianity, which left me cold until I encountered it in another language other than English. This brings me to Vira.

Vira took my hand firmly and, at just twenty-three years old, said to me, her new friend, twenty-nine, "You don't need medication. We will now pray for your healing." Her face was radiant, her eyes glowing, and her motions sure. I clearly remember thinking, "So this was what Christianity looks like from the inside . . ."

The spreading of Christianity on the premise of salvation—*have you been saved?*—pained me after my liberal studies education at Sonoma State, which is why I'm a major fan of Christian higher education. I'm all about the integration of faith and learning. I think it may be especially the case that I love combining all aspects of life as a student. I will probably always be a student because it is just such a hopeful enterprise, provided it's in a Christian context and provided we aren't making ourselves God as we study the things of God (it's always a risk).

If I struggled with the spreading aspect of Christianity in my early twenties, this was because I hadn't yet met Russian and Ukrainian Evangelicals. Russian, a seamless language whose urgency speaks to the heart and not the mind, freed me from the stiff world of biblical English, a language which, I would say after reflecting on my own personal experience in my twenties as an outsider, bars non-Christian and formerly Christian Americans from the faith. Just the word "righteous" in English sends shudders down the secular spine, so judgmental does it sound. In Russian, however, Christianity was made new for me for it entered through the heart for once and not the mind.

I shared with Vira that I had been hospitalized, that I was scared, exhausted, and didn't know how to teach anymore. Nothing felt relevant. Before being hospitalized I had been a fighter. I was going to show everyone that I wasn't crazy, that I wasn't going to sue them, and, toward the end, that I didn't need medication.

I had never missed work.

Now I had missed two weeks without even telling my boss where I was going or that I would be gone.

When I got back to school two weeks later it was surreal. It was the first time I had been out of the daily grind in my life. It made me realize that life would go on without me. That someday I would die, that schools would still be alternately in session and on break, that people would continue to get married and get divorced, and that people would be born and would die. All without me here on earth. It was unreal. The only thing I can liken it to is when you get rear-ended and you pull over to the side of the road. The other cars keep driving and you are astounded that time has not stopped altogether.

Vira promised me her church would pray for my healing. She wouldn't say what had happened to me, but, she said, she would share that I was sick. Years later, when my dearest mentor and friend, a professor at SPU, asked if I was okay and if he could pray for me, I just said, "I'm sick." The Ukrainian church in the Pacific Northwest that I found when I first met up with Vira's friends up north, had a prayer time at my first meeting with them and I said, "ya bol'na," "I'm sickly." And they held me in prayer. You see, with other prayer requests you say, "Please pray for this to shrink the tumor," or, "God, help the labor to go smoothly." No one ever shares to the entire church, "Please help me stop thinking my house is bugged."

Vira's faith grounded her so that where most people would have run, she approached. I felt like a leper being given a new life and clear skin when she took my hand. She spoke right into my soul, and it was clear that the LORD was with her. I was renewed, awestruck, and my heart began to sing through the deadening medications.

"We will be praying for your healing, Erin."

When you are suffering, such a promise of healing, said with faith and resolution, gives life. But only when given with love. I have had friends who walk with a limp be approached by Christians who want to push their prayer life onto them and "heal" them. It is a pain-inducing shaming that results as you are singled out on the bus surrounded by Bibles and encircled by self-righteous people out to "fix" you without your having asked for it as you miss your bus stop. Great, still longer to walk, with difficulty, the long road to work.

Yes, healings only work when given with love, where there is trust, in private, and while walking a tightrope of tentative mutuality. And I received faith, hope, and love in addition to the promise of healing from my dear new friend Vira. I received this in Russian, and so my critical English-speaking thoughts had surrendered themselves to the prayerful assurances uttered with conviction in Russian.

Through Vira and her assurance of my healing, I began to gain an inkling that Christianity still breathed. Hope replaced the blackness of despair after I got out of the hospital, and I contemplated the prospect of being healed by faith. Maybe it was prayer that was needed. I had been attracted to someone outside of my marriage; maybe that was God's punishing me and I got a mental illness as a result. Now that I have been reformed, I told myself, I don't need medicine. My character is intact . . . this means I still can have children! I don't need medication. I need Jesus! I've learned my lesson!

I began to live with one foot in fundamentalism while continuing to live the other in Black Lives Matter Queer Alliance activism. To this day I believe that my mind being on the schizophrenia spectrum has helped my ability to immerse myself in other languages, cultures, and religious perspectives.

Foreign and yet familiar, Ukrainian Christianity—not Orthodoxy but Protestantism—renewed me where nothing else had. No American-minded person had reached out and given theological hope. The doctor who had given hope and bumped me up on an antidepressant while removing my mood stabilizer had given hope. See how well that worked? It's like with each failure of care and connection, I was losing hope for life, let alone normalcy.

But Vira was different. Vira abided with the LORD and the LORD with Vira. And together, in Russian, they made space for me. I sought refuge in the LORD and Jesus. Augustine writes, "your dwelling in God means that you are held by him, God's dwelling in you means he holds you, lest you fall." This is true . . . God holds you, lest you fall . . . Unless you go off your medicine because you are convinced that God will keep you from falling as you do so.

Such lessons are learned the hard way.

Even harder to understand is that it works out well for some people. These are the most painful people for me to be around, because they think that what worked for them will work for you. I have a former tutoring student whose parent survived stage four cancer and wrote a book on how to beat cancer based on diet alone. Clearly a healthy diet is possibly one of the best things we can invest in when living with chronic ailments, but the idea that you could follow his advice, advice that worked for *his* unique situation, and come out cancer-free is not scientifically possible, and such advice could be dangerous. Telling people what worked for us will work for another person is like selling snake oil. It occurs to me that people may be reading this who are medicine resistant. I hope I'm not heaping on the pain if that applies to you. It took me five years to get on the right medicine and eight to find the right supplement that made me (almost) normal, so all I can say is don't give up. Perhaps even that message would be disheartening for some, though. For which I apologize. I'll just reiterate that I acknowledge that I am not my readers and that what works for me may not work for you. My prayer is that my sharing my life with you might help you find your own path.

Anyway, I went off my medicine and I fell harder than the last time. The delusions, which had departed on my high dosage of the antipsychotic, had been "healed" and "cured," and so I went off the antipsychotic.

A week later I called Todd: "Todd! I'm scared! I am certain you are trying to kill me. If I hadn't just gotten out of the hospital and been told I was crazy, there would be nothing that would keep me from believing that you would kill me right now!"

Todd left work immediately. I was in the shower trying to calm down when he arrived. He opened the door, and I could hear that he had opened it because the alarm had beeped. But he did not enter. My mind raced. Does he have an axe? Is he going to try to kill me while I'm in the shower? Is it someone else?

He later confided, years later, when I had been well for a long time, that he hadn't come in because he had been scared. Terrified, in fact. Sometimes in the middle of the night I can't sleep and I get up to write or pray or to take communion (which I serve to myself sometimes when I'm down or feeling spiritually attacked). When I do this, he gets extremely scared. He can't share his worries fully, because he doesn't want to hurt me, but I imagine that it's fear that his wife has lost her mind again. It must be an isolating experience since he can't even share it with his soulmate without her feeling like a failure. As a result, I am such a good wife and I try to do everything just right. I've probably missed out on writing two whole books in the last couple years just out of a desire to stay in bed and not trigger him in the middle of the night when I feel inspired.

How would you feel thinking that your wife is crazy enough to think that you are going to kill her, and entering the house with a woman in it who had run into the emergency room just months before and been involuntarily committed? People who think they're going to be attacked are far more likely to lash out.

Todd came in while I sat on the ground in the shower, and he sat down outside the shower, talking to me patiently. He talked me out of my thinking. He is so sweet with me, always patient, and so sincere. He really engages me when I'm having a hard time, as if I'd never had an illness ever. I am his equal. I know the psychosis in this moment was triggered because I was on my way up to 200 milligrams of the antidepressant with a low dose of the antipsychotic. That same doctor had wanted to prove to her other colleague that it hadn't been the antidepressant the last time that had caused it.

"Should we call the doctor?" Todd asked, after I had regained my wits.

"No." I had said. "I think that by bringing up the delusions and then counteracting them we are curing those parts of my brain. Let's keep working through it."

Three days later the police stopped me as I walked across a busy street to hang myself at the river because I was convinced that Todd had never loved me and that he had been paid to stay with me by the government who wanted to watch me to make sure I never became a terrorist.[1] Todd drove me to the hospital and acted natural, and I wondered why his mom was following in the car behind us.

Obviously because he had been terrified. My poor husband, the love of my life, feared his own wife. Nothing makes me sadder than to think of the isolation that he must have experienced. It was unnecessary isolation. If I hadn't been so eager to get off of the antipsychotics we could have lived in the same loving bubble of reality. That was eight years ago, and I haven't been off of the medicine since. For the first several years after resolving to always take medicine, as my faith got stronger, I would think maybe God had cured me. But then I remember what Todd has already been through, that I want to foster children today, and I know that I will never go off of my medicine. When you are unwell, you get used to being unwell after a point and then sickness becomes normalized. So then you think, "What the heck, maybe I can go off of my medicine just a little bit." But if you ask a person who had never had mental health issues, "If I told you that in the next three years, you'll have been hospitalized twice, once involuntarily, that you'll almost lose your life and your marriage, and that you might be thinking that you've been falsely accused of being a terrorist for the rest of your life, would you take a pill to stop it?" I swear, you'd have to be insane not to take the pill.

---

1. Do not kill yourself. Call 988 Suicide and Crisis Lifeline. Never give up.

I read the depth psychology books, or the pop Christian psychology books that use "mental illness" in "scare quotes." Look at the mental health charts in my basement and then tell me that "mental illness" belongs in "scare quotes."

In Christian circles, especially more traditional ones, it is a fact that Jesus doesn't just save; with salvation we are healed. This conviction, I believe, inspires hope where often there is none. That was the case with me. And then when it didn't work out the ground fell out from under me. It created despair deeper than just being a human with an illness. I was a human who was unloved by God, unworthy of Jesus's love since I hadn't been healed. "Your faith has healed you . . ." Then does this mean I don't have enough faith? I never had an affair. If I had then I probably would have reasoned that I had been damned to all eternity even though God is a forgiving and loving and merciful God.

Real healings really happen. People take risks that they would not otherwise take to live without medicine. And for some, this really works. It took me corresponding with a moral and historical theologian to realize that healing can include medicine. It's not always required, some people just recover, but medical science cooperates with God's grace in the lives of those who suffer. Read my book *Emergent Grace* for information on how to thrive with serious mental illness in a way that encourages medication and therapy. I don't resent Vira, and we're still friends. She gave me hope and that hope has stayed with me, bolstered by theological education that honors evolution, the ordination and equality of women, and use of medicine.

The way God designed our bodies is a model for understanding our lives together as a church: every part dependent on every other part, the parts we mention and the parts we don't, the parts we see and the parts we don't. If one part hurts, every other part is involved in the hurt, and in the healing. If one part flourishes, every other part enters into the exuberance.

—1 Cor 12:25–26

7

Therapy and Medication

Almighty God, who has promised to hear the petitions
Of those who ask in your Son's Name:
We beseech you mercifully to incline your ear to us
who have now made our prayers and supplications unto you;
And grant that those things which we
have faithfully asked according to your will,
May effectually be obtained, to the relief of our necessity,
and to the setting forth of your glory;
through Jesus Christ our LORD. *Amen.*

—*THE BOOK OF COMMON PRAYER*

PRAYER AND DISCERNMENT ARE arts, and I think that in my case they are interrelated to therapy and medication, which enhance my ability to pray, discern, and act. I can still remember my twenties when I *began* having a hard time but wasn't living with psychosis yet. This was the so-called "prodromal" period. I started going to a therapist, who told me that I should tell him my worries and then, crucially, he taught me how to see my thoughts as though they were a leaf floating down a stream. I was supposed to watch the thought from the shores rather than identify with it. In other words, I was being taught the important lesson that we are not our thoughts.

Therapists call the process of overidentifying with your thoughts, fusion. And so, their job is to help us defuse from our thoughts, and then, if we're lucky to have a good therapist, they train us how to defuse those thoughts ourselves. If you have schizophrenia, this can be especially difficult, and you may need to continue seeing a therapist in order to keep perspective on how you are not your thinking. I'm not a professional, but that's what happened with me.

It was an important lesson when I first learned to watch my thinking rather than experiencing my thoughts as facts. I remember feeling so relaxed after it for several days. I realized it was my interpretation that was causing the distress. I had attached values to events, and these values weren't universal. Eventually, I needed to go on medicine to remind myself that I was not my thinking because, over time, my thinking became more persuasive to myself even as it became more detached from logic. And it became so strong that I created the situations I feared were happening in my interpretive world as I alienated myself from friends and family and coworkers.

Now, safely on my medicine and avoiding things and situations that are triggering when I can—choosing my battles, if you will—I stay on the bank and watch the leaves of my thinking pass by on the streams of life.

Mind, body, and soul are all one in the Christian faith, though we do talk about them as different things and they are, in fact, distinct (though interconnected). Our bodies resurrect with our souls. This claim is scriptural, though perhaps also controversial. I believe in the sanctified imagination and that, drawing upon our sanctified imaginations, we can see in our mind's eye that body and soul are knitted together, starting with conception. There's even a psalm that talks about how we are knitted together in our mothers' wombs and how God is there.

I remember one of the most poignant sermons on racial justice that I ever heard was on how our physical bodies are there with us in heaven, resurrecting with our souls, and how this means that colorblind theology that stresses we are all the same and that race doesn't matter is a threat to authentic Christian community.

The moral of the story was that God makes us intentionally, with attention to skin color and other physical features, and those are resurrected with us. I'm not sure how I would bring that conception into contact with rare genetic disorders or cancers which, I pray, in heaven, their sufferers will be liberated from. Sometimes sermons can make complex things too simple. My brain is fragile. I hope I don't live with psychosis in heaven.

The mind, as I imagine it, is the nexus of body and soul. Scripture tells us to renew our minds with the Word of God. In my book *Emergent Grace*, I talk about a book called *Truth Therapy* and how it is specifically focused on getting to the soul through the mind. This book is great, and I like books in general because I can put them down whenever I'm triggered, while I can't just run out of a therapist's office usually. I mean, I'm sure I *could*, and I have *wanted to* before, but I don't usually do this. In fact, I never have.

Through the soul we can access the mind and body, and sexual abuse affects all three. The very life force. Sex is the force that brings forth new life and rekindles connection in a vibrant marital relationship, which is also life-giving (with reservations, for example: I was abstinent a whole year while married due to *likely false* memories of rape). Healing practitioners who heal via somatic (in other words, body) work are amazing, but unless they have wisdom, they fall into the trap that teaches that if you can't heal somatically, then you can't heal. They can talk about how all other healing modalities fail because they don't access the body's wisdom. I disagree.

Really, there are as many types of healing as there are types of people. And sometimes, we must acknowledge that it's not about healing but about transforming our idea of what healing means.

Healing does not always mean cured.

I cannot be cured of schizoaffective disorder. But I can heal myself by not judging myself. My medicine can heal me and bring me peace and the ability to experience joy. And right now, that is enough. I am committed to staying on my antipsychotics, which heal me when I take them every day.

Polyvagal theory, developed in 1994 and refined over the years by Stephen Porges, describes the importance of the vagus nerve, especially in the context of trauma. The vagus nerve goes from the head to the torso, and it regulates our fight, flight, freeze, or fawn response (the fawn one was news to me when I first read about it, but it's basically when you're so traumatized that you suck up to your abuser or potential abuser; in fact, that is my own go-to trauma response since I have complex PTSD). By working on the body, we can heal the mind . . . or so the story goes. This is true, but much more complicated, in my experience, as a sufferer with psychosis.

Practitioners vary widely in skill, faith tradition, and . . . motivation. Some unconsciously discharge their own trauma into their clients. The woman who did my body therapy, I already mentioned, probably implanted false rape memories in me. Be very careful about who you let touch your body. Check their credentials, check their character, and get multiple references.

Touching someone and then claiming to know the history of their body's trauma is spiritual and professional malpractice as far as I'm concerned, and professional mental health workers I have talked to specifically about my therapeutic relationship with the body worker have agreed. The woman who treated me also told me that she was raped by her father, which is an astounding self-disclosure in a therapeutic setting, and definitely unprofessional to share. So what I think happened was she projected that onto me, and then physically programmed it into me though physical touch. Given that my mental boundaries were so low due to ongoing psychosis and my inability to reality test, I just sort of absorbed it, just like I had absorbed the trauma of the film as a graduate student. Which is why I believe it is very important to be treated by professionals, and professionals who are licensed and clinically trained *to do the work they will be doing on you.* I will only work with people who understand psychosis. In other words, I don't go to a massage therapist for psychosis treatments anymore. I rely on medicine and what I call boundary work. I do have a massage therapist healer I go to, and it does help regulate my mood and psychosis, but she only touches my head and feet, doesn't offer any interpretations, and is extremely emotionally mature. I don't share my inner anguish with her. Or my joys.

I've had the same mental health therapist for six years now and he also prescribes my medications. He is a psychiatrist (an MD) with a PhD in psychology. He is trained in dialectical behavioral therapy, so he knows not to attach to the ideas I come to him with, and he holds space and listens without judgment. He is calm and kayaks, acting as a professional guide on weekends. However, he also is not Christian and sometimes gives me advice that doesn't resonate with my Christian worldview, which I don't follow. This has led me to only use him for therapy for emergencies and to rely chiefly on his medication management. This is pretty doable since antipsychotics can get rid of a lot of the anxiety and paranoia that accompany the occasionally distressed inner lives of people with serious mental health challenges. (Everyone is different. What works for me may not work for you, though it might. Seek professional input.)

I know some individuals with untreated serious mental illness who people frequently ask me (as if I'm the expert on all mentally ill people since I'm mentally ill) if I could get them to go to therapy. I always think to myself, if they have what I have, then therapy is not going to cut it. People with psychosis benefit from antipsychotics. Some people, not me, can get to the point where they need less medicine because they do talk therapy and the therapist talks them out of delusions. That does not work for me. I imagine the therapist to be part of the delusion.

Regarding people with serious mental illness who are not me: it has taken me a long time to realize that not all mentally ill people are the same. Some people are bad or mean or abusive, even without mental illness. Therefore, it follows, that there can be bad, mean, or abusive mentally ill people. Initially I trusted mentally ill people more because I thought they would be like me. Some of us, indeed most I know, are so wonderful because of what we've been through. We're like a little club gleefully reflecting on how we've made it through when we're feeling good, and consoling one another on a deep, sustaining level on the hard days. I try to remind myself that people are people first and foremost, regardless of race, ethnicity, disability status, immigration status, and other aspects. Everyone is different, even those of us who have similar ailments. I also try to see the good in everyone and try not to think of people as evil.

❖❖❖

THERAPY AND MEDICATION

Why would you ever complain, O Jacob,
or, whine, Israel, saying,
"God has lost track of me.
He doesn't care what happens to me"?
Don't you know anything? Haven't you been listening?
God doesn't come and go. God lasts.
He's Creator of all you can see or imagine.
He doesn't get tired out, doesn't pause to catch his breath.
And he knows everything, inside and out.
He energizes those who get tired,
gives fresh strength to dropouts.
For even young people tire and drop out,
young folk in their prime stumble and fall.
But those who wait upon God get fresh strength.
They spread their wings and soar like eagles,
They run and don't get tired,
they walk and don't lag behind.

—Isa 40:27–31

8

Exercise, Physical and Spiritual

O God, in the course of this busy life,
give us times of refreshment and peace;
And grant that we may so use our leisure to rebuild
our bodies and renew our minds,
That our spirits may be opened to the goodness of your creation;
through Jesus Christ our LORD.
Amen.

—*THE BOOK OF COMMON PRAYER*

I'M AWARE THAT SOME readers, even without antipsychotics, may
have very shapely bodies. That is beautiful. I'm aware that some
readers may be differently abled and physically unable to do any
physical exercise. You matter. Some may have had to deal with
exercise addiction or body dysmorphia. You are appreciated. That
said, people often think I'm pregnant. I get knowing smiles from
moms, preferential seating sometimes, and other things that, were
I pregnant, I'm sure would be very touching. When I was twenty-
something and losing what I thought was my career at the time,
there seemed to be only one alternative to becoming a professor:
dying. I took meds and survived. Now I have come to the point that
I no longer identify with my looks, I no longer identify with my

career, and all I want to do is help people. I know people in their sixties and seventies who are not even this motivated to serve others. Some people never grow up.

Our culture values outcome-based exercise. You exercise to look good. Of course, looking good, if we are to follow society's definition (which I don't), doesn't mean toned legs and body. It means thinness. I am not flabby because I exercise daily; and yet still, despite myself, for a long time this wasn't "good enough" for me. I wanted to keep being thin.

Some people have embraced what they call being "fat." They have reclaimed the term. My fear of doing that is that I would lose the motivation to exercise. See how it's a vicious cycle? If you've embraced the "fat" term, reclaiming it, good for you. I've done all the mind games with myself on how to exercise without expecting "thin" results. So far it's working for me. When I do my straight-arm knee tucks, I can feel my thigh and stomach touching, which is not something I can usually ignore, and which, without my antipsychotics, would not be the case, and sometimes I get discouraged. But then I remember I'm exercising and that I have a body that is quite functional and I am reminded to actively, quite intentionally, cultivate gratitude for what is working for me. It's a matter of what I focus on. Do I want to focus on my stomach and thigh touching while I pull my knee under my belly, or do I want to focus on how my hip works beautifully and that I am able to hold my weight with my arms?

My husband and I have learned that at this stage he is very affirming of my beauty and says that he just cares if I'm healthy. He is very, very supportive of me taking my medicine because our shared quality of life is like night and day whether I'm off or on my medicine. Also, when I was on less medicine for a year, I lost weight, and he did not compliment me on my figure, likely because he knew I would probably have to go up on it again. He is very intentional about noticing my beautiful body, mind, and soul and not attaching it to my actual size.

Just last week I turned thirty-eight (I'm writing this mid-May, my birthday is May 5). My husband got me clothes. Let's just say he knows never to do that ever again. The clothes he got me didn't fit me, even though it was a larger size. I had just been writing about weight and fat-shaming in our culture for this book (the above paragraphs). I had thought I had a handle on it and had a sense of mastery over my insecurity about my weight . . . Let's just say that I still don't have a grip on the shame of being overweight on some days. My birthday was one such day. I completely lost it.

I don't want to pay a totally rosy picture; some people are so overweight that they can't walk, and antipsychotics can make people who don't have a good baseline metabolism even heavier than me. There is no way to say this except that I hope that you can work with your doctors and a good therapist to be as emotionally and physically healthy as possible, and that you don't hate yourself. I'm praying for all of us in this situation, that we would find peace and joy amidst the hardships of weight gain and fat shaming in a culture obsessed with thinness. You are God's child, you are beautiful, and you matter. You are so important. I'm praying for you. For all of us.

I have been on antipsychotics since 2012, but I went off them for the year 2014–15 because they were affecting my teaching ability and my students were thinking I was pregnant (I can't have kids due to my medicine, but there's a hope-filled essay on adoption in my appendix by my friend Stacie). I had become ashamed. When I was hospitalized in early 2015 (having been off antipsychotics for seven months and having decompensated during that time), they wanted to put me back on the medicine I had been on from 2012–13. I was vehement that I did *not* want to be on it due to weight gain. So, they said I should take a different medication, without saying that it was also an antipsychotic.

Well, it worked! And way better than the initial antipsychotic. Different drugs work differently for different people. Experiment (with professional supervision). I didn't know it was an antipsychotic at the time, and wouldn't have taken it if I *had* known, but once I took it and I was no longer paranoid and delusional, there was no going back. I have been on it ever since. I was so grateful to feel safe in my head and to have the ability to have relationships that I thought, no way am I going off this ever again!

I live a very privileged life. I exercise every morning, while others do not have the luxury of time (or health) to do so. I do strength training. I breathe heavily when I walk because my medicine affects my central nervous system (and because I'm overweight), but I still walk. At first my husband was worried about my health because I pant on hills, but now we know that exercising is important and so we just deal with my labored breathing. Getting out in nature is important for your mental, physical, and spiritual health.

Just like there is physical exercise, there is spiritual exercise. In fact, in the history of Christianity there were the "spiritual exercises" developed by Saint Ignatius of Loyola (1491–1556). These exercises feature an array of prayers, meditations, and contemplative practices. My spiritual director is a devout, but very accepting of Protestants, Catholic and she talks about corporal acts of mercy, which are the fruit of personal investment in the spiritual exercises. Basically, you work on yourself and practice prayer, Christian reflection, and such elements of spiritual growth and then, as an outpouring of having a spiritually fruitful personal relationship with God, you can serve others in the way that Mother Teresa did.

Some of my earliest and most joyful childhood memories are of reading the Bible. I went to a variety of church groups as a child, and already shared that in high school I even played keyboard and sang prominently in my youth group church services. I still read the Bible whenever I can, though sometimes I take a month off from this practice, repenting every time since the Bible helps me be a better and more balanced person. Reading the Bible is tricky and I don't want to just blindly advocate the practice. You need the right lens for Bible study. Not all lenses are equal. Read my book *Emergent Grace* for more on this topic and how Bible study affects my mental health. Suffice to say that if after reading the Bible I feel more judgmental, I know I have been reading it wrong. We read the Bible to judge ourselves, not others. And, equally important, we read the Bible not only to be better but also to know that we are loved as we are, and that we are also forgiven and should forgive, provided that it's psychologically and physically safe to do so. Abuse can be cyclical and so if it's a pattern of abuse it's not always safe to return. Maybe the abuser is just having a good week and it will get dangerous again when they start having a bad time. This should be taken into account with forgiveness. What are the patterns and structures of a relationship (see my afterword for more information, since it was written by a pastor, professor and theologian about this very quandary).

In 2013, I was teaching at my former high school in Sacramento and met a Ukrainian woman who was a teacher's aide, and with whom I conversed in Russian often at work (Vira, who I discussed above and who encouraged a faith healing). We became friends outside of work. Through her, I started reading the Bible in Russian, and it did not have the judgmental overtones that I associated with it in English readings. For some reason, unconsciously, I associated the Bible with hate and foolishness and—no offense, I'm just being honest—white missionaries, and colonialism in English. (For the record, I'm currently getting a Master of Divinity in Missional Leadership, where we learn how to do crosscultural missions more responsibly.)

In Russian the Bible was so beautiful and spiritual. The Russian language is my favorite language, even in this political climate. It doesn't have articles (words like "the" or "a") and each word can end in a variety of twelve ways if it's a noun. Most verbs have two forms, some radically different from one another. It's a complicated language, but when you speak it well it goes right into the soul because it's not as wordy and full of articles as other languages. I still get so much joy out of reading the Bible in Russian—see the appendix for my translation from modern Russian into English of the first chapter of the book of James.

I have even thought of offering up a translation of the New Testament, translating it from modern Russian into English so people can get a Russian Protestant feel (my friend is Ukrainian Baptist fundamentalist) of the gospel message, minus the part of her culture that doesn't believe in evolution, the ordination of women, or that men and women can be equals in relationships. Bible study was extremely painful for me as a person with a mental illness before I met my friend.

Spiritual Bible reading, which is different from Bible study, is my go-to remedy for demonic attacks. I know! Wild that I actually believe in this sort of thing since I'm a little progressive (!), but I've experienced this specifically and so I know it's real. I read the Bible aloud when I'm feeling spiritually attacked or when I have relationship challenges, and it helps a great deal. I especially recommend reading the Bible aloud. Not only does it slow you down but, if you do believe that mental illness is possibly associated with evil "spirits of the air," then this is a way to combat them.

I remember the first time I did this. I was in my office and I felt an evil spirit there. Overwhelmed, I took out the Bible and started reading it from the beginning toward the end, starting in the Old Testament. I read it out loud. When I got to the section about worshiping false idols—actually, there are many such sections—I paused and remembered that I had put a tarot card in my office because I had liked the picture. It was about laying the groundwork as an artist (in my case, I hoped it would inspire my writing). Immediately I came and took the card and put it in the trash out of my home. I read the Bible for several more hours and eventually I felt the presence of my mentor's daughter who had just died (read my book *Emergent Grace* for more on my mentor, who was the one who got me to see taking medicine can be in keeping with God's will and not a lack of faith) and, for nearly a year, she was with me in my life, guiding me as a guardian angel. She is still my guardian angel. For a year she was with me experiencing life with me as a spiritual companion, but then on Good Friday 2019 I had a dream where she rose, bodily, into the heavens. She hasn't been with me on an hourly basis since. This is a blessing because it means she worked through her spiritual blockages. I like to think I helped her just as she helped me.

> Don't make idols for yourselves; don't set up an image or a
> sacred pillar for yourselves, and don't place a carved stone
> in your land that you can bow down to in worship. I am
> God, your God.

—Lev 26:1

9

Purpose and Disability

Heavenly Father, we remember before you
those who suffer want and anxiety from lack of work.
Guide the people of this land so to use our public and private wealth
that all may find suitable and fulfilling employment,
And receive just payment for their labor;
Through Jesus Christ our LORD. Amen.

— *THE BOOK OF COMMON PRAYER*

I HAVE REALIZED THAT rather than goal attainment and goal setting, I want my goals to be qualitative: I want to always show love. That is my goal. But it's not a striving thing. It's an existence thing. It has been an interesting journey to where I am now, and I definitely think that my life is richer now and my experiences more meaningful than they were when I was an ambitious and successful twenty-something. When I interact with friends who are still on the success treadmill, I do so with a mix of admiration for them and their efforts, and a complex gratitude, both that they are making a mark on the world, and that that life is no longer for me, unless you count my life as an author and speaker. I try to not identify with my roles anymore, however, even as a writer and speaker. This is because if I ever lose my ability to write and speak, I want to embody the truth that we are all equal, regardless of how we perform in this life. We are all created *and remain* of equal worth in the eyes of God, and I try to see us all as equal and fundamentally the same even amidst the great diversity of life and abilities on this planet.

A matter of perspective is what it is. When I was first getting off the success treadmill, I was desperately sad and anxious and worried that I was losing all the accolades I had earned. And I had worked hard and genuinely earned them. But as I came to understand who I am and how I was to live now, and as I came to embrace that and to welcome when I was feeling good and accept when I was doing poorly with hopes it wouldn't last long, I found that the times when I was doing poorly were less frequent, not only because I was no longer assessing them as times when I was doing poorly but also because my self-hatred had greatly diminished.

When I'm not doing well, I read about people who have struggled and overcome.

Reading about people of purpose inspires me.

Ever since I was thirteen, I have loved the work of Richard Wright. When I was in English class my sophomore year of high school, we read *Black Boy* and, inspired by this harrowing autobiographical study, I read several major works by civil rights activists. Wright, however, was the most impactful because he also was a scholar of language. Deeply moved by his love of learning I began keeping word journals that would spiral into the massive Russian-German and Russian-English dictionaries, hundreds of pages long, that I made in order to master those languages as an undergraduate and graduate student.

Surviving my childhood was my purpose for many years. And then recovering from it became my purpose. And then fighting racism and colonialism became, and remains, my purpose (I even have an essay on decolonial ways of thinking about environmentalism in the appendix—check it out!). My family (we are a white family) was not politically active in civil rights, but we also were not bigoted. My high school was a predominantly white, affluent, suburban public high school in Sacramento. It was colorblind Democrat-leaning—obviously colorblindness is now problematic—with a rogue Republican Ayn-Rand-loving economics teacher who also taught world history. If it weren't for the individual books in the library that I encountered from my high school, I would not have had the civil rights education that I did. It is something that is ongoing for me, to this day. My mom's favorite story regarding my racial identity development was when I went to ballet and met my first African-American friend. I was obsessed with the color of her cheeks, Mom tells me now. I just thought she was the most beautiful person I had ever seen. Of course, this shows that I lived a sheltered, white-neighborhood life, doesn't it?

I grew up with socioeconomic privilege and was able to access medication and therapy at a young age, starting, also, at thirteen years old, when my parents began the four-year process of divorcing. They lived next door to one another in two side-by-side two-story houses in a cul-de-sac and I built the fence between their houses (initially they had just bought their neighbor's house and turned their old one into an office for my dad). I went from an honors student freshman year to a D-student in sophomore year during the divorce. As already mentioned, this definitely impacted my college choices, since I applied to the UCs and was rejected, going to a state school—Sonoma State University—for my first two years of college before transferring to UC Berkeley. For this reason, as well, I no longer am impressed when I hear people have gone to impressive schools or have had a distinguished career. I'm more impressed by character in the face of adversity, and there are people of all stations of life, some who didn't even finish elementary school, with quality character, strong inner purpose, and higher social vision. When I was doing extremely well in terms of prestige and accolades, I thought that everyone on earth wanted to do exactly what I was doing and that, therefore, I was one in a million. Turns out, yes, I'm one in a million, but that so is everyone else! Not everyone wants to hire a stellar student. For wise employers, the ability to cultivate and sustain relationships and the ability to sacrifice one's own standing for the needs of the group may be more important and valuable. Were I in a position to hire people, I would sure value character above intellect. My therapist once told me never to put knowledge above wisdom. This is so true!

Before becoming a writer, I struggled to find my purpose after healing from child abuse. I read something recently that said that to be a meaningful contributor you have to be consistent. This is certainly true to a point. But I think it has been crucial for me to realize that if when I try my best, and make it clear up front that I have a disability—sometimes I don't share what it is—that keeps me from being consistent and that, therefore, I want to know how to be involved in a way that plays to that . . . I think that if you do that then it is possible to contribute without being consistent. I just don't sign up for roles that require consistency.

Now as a writer, I find that I have been blessed with the ability to consistently write.

Often, when not doing well, I tell myself: don't forget you are *always* a contributor. Just by existing you matter. God created us all equal and we are all fully human, no matter how broken we may feel. Or be.

I tell myself: don't forget that sharing your story, when it is safe to, and when it is not traumatic to do so, is a contribution that will allow for others to feel like they can share theirs. I have made myself ill with worry after sharing, so I went easy on myself and didn't hire a publicist with my first book so I could take care of myself. I may hire a publicist in the future if I continue to do well and have a clearer sense of my brand over time, however.

I tell myself: don't forget that you are a contributor, and you matter, every time you pray for and think of others.

A MEDITATION . . .

What if we looked at our lives in terms of degrees of contribution rather than degrees of wellness or illness?

What if the scale by which we assess our worth is not based on how we are doing, but how we are contributing?

If we did this, then we would have to rethink what it means to contribute. I just went to a women's retreat, where I led some meditations and taught about racial justice. One of my co-presenters led a presentation on our bodies and how to link body, heart, and mind together (see the appendix).

She led a gratitude meditation.

During this meditation, I was able to visualize my dog who just died, my grandma who died several years ago, my uncle who died in April last year, and several other dear times of my life that I tend to remember with despair because I lost my initial career when mental health issues came up.

All I had was gratitude for them. Usually, I think about them through a lens of loss and tragedy.

Lenses matter, and I can think of my life in terms of degrees of contribution rather than in terms of the profound losses that I have suffered.

Right now, my contribution is as a wife, daughter, and pray-er, and also, I donate to places. I am a substitute teacher and a tutor.

Rather than thinking about how I used to contribute more as a teacher in a PhD program, or as a high school teacher, or as someone who was planning on becoming a mother, I can think about how the lives I touched as a teacher are touched even though it was in the past and I can't teach anymore. How when I foster children in the future, I will be mothering them even though I can't have my own, and that I can mentor as a tutor. And how I teach with my life as a blogger, author, and web developer at biblespanish.com.

I just lived through a rough patch for the last couple of months, though it was nothing like my first years of illness. It was much more manageable this time around. Rather than thinking of it that way, however, I can think that my life itself is a contribution because I pray for others, I was still writing, and I submitted this book manuscript for publication, and it was accepted.

Even when I'm not well, I pray. And you can, too.

That is the best contribution of all, and it is accessible to everyone. If you are not feeling well, try it out: think in terms of degrees of contribution rather than how you're doing.

Think about degrees of contribution rather than degrees of wellness or illness.

You matter. Contribute mindfully. Contribute meaningfully.

Pray. For yourself and for others.

But what happens when we live God's way? He brings gifts into our lives, much the same way that fruit appears in an orchard—things like affection for others, exuberance about life, serenity. We develop a willingness to stick with things, a sense of compassion in the heart, and a conviction that a basic holiness permeates things and people. We find ourselves involved in loyal commitments, not needing to force our way in life, able to marshal and direct our energies wisely. Legalism is helpless in bringing this about; it only gets in the way. Among those who belong to Christ, everything connected with getting our own way and mindlessly responding to what everyone else calls necessities is killed off for good—crucified.

—Gal 5:22–24

10

Familial Justice and Social Decoloniality

O God the Father of our LORD Jesus Christ,
our only Savior, the Prince of Peace:
Give us grace seriously to lay to heart the great dangers
we are in by our unhappy divisions;
Take away all hatred and prejudice,
and whatever else may hinder us from
Godly union and concord;
that, as there is but one Body and one Spirit,
One hope of our calling, one LORD, one Faith, one Baptism,
one God and Father of us all,
So we may be all of one heart and of one soul,
United in one holy bond of truth and peace,
of faith and charity, and may
With one mind and one mouth glorify thee;
Through Jesus Christ our LORD. Amen.

—*THE BOOK OF COMMON PRAYER*

FOR SEVERAL YEARS I did not talk to my dad because I thought he had raped me and I had memories of it. Now, of course, I'm not so sure and tend to think those were false memories implanted by a therapist. Some therapists have tried to latch onto these memories as proof, but a wise doctor once told me to fire therapists who do that, because they are trying to make an ambiguous past concrete in a way that could amplify my psychosis.

False memories of rape aside, there was, however, also something else that prompted me to remove myself from Dad's presence. I had been studying boundaries. I learned that I could only control my own behavior in any given relationship, and that I could remove myself from negative behavior as an independent adult. This discovery was huge for me. As a dependent child I could not remove myself. As dependent adults in a domestic violence situation, we cannot always remove ourselves. But I could remove myself as an adult.

Specifically, I had learned about the domestic abuse wheel, which is a graphic that details the eight means of abuse in domestic violence:

1. Economic abuse
2. Coercion and threats
3. Intimidation
4. Emotional abuse
5. Male privilege
6. Using children
7. Minimizing, denying, and blaming
8. Using isolation

The hub of the graphic (you can look up "abuse wheel" in Google Images) reads, "Power and Control" and the above numbered items are encircled with the words "Physical and Sexual Violence." It's important to say that women can be violent and that men can also be victims of abuse. I want to be clear.

I don't want to get into my mom's relationship with Dad, since that is her story to tell and since Dad has reformed and I don't want to focus on the negative, but let's just say Dad used some of these against us. I shared the graphic with him right after I had gotten out of my second hospitalization, and he was so surprised, and I told him I wouldn't interact with him if he continued to joke about violence. I also asked him not to minimize what I had gone through (joking about violence also minimizes it). Basically, I gave him three tries to behave in a way that respected my autonomy and agency and valued my lived experience of abuse, and he couldn't do it. In fact, his intimidation and coercive efforts increased dramatically, even though I was twenty-nine and he couldn't do anything about controlling me. Now it was about controlling the very narrative of my life. He got to share his side with the family and was believed, while I was isolated from family and urged to return to family events. No one believed me, and I received steep pressure not to publish this book. I am still trying to regain the intimate relationships with them that I had had before my three-year hiatus from family events. It's sad that just by honestly recounting the past, some people in unhealthy families are made out to be victimizers of the people who actually did the harm.

Can't you forgive? I was actually told by a family member when I shared I was publishing this work that I should read my Bible more, because Jesus forgave. I was clear: I have forgiven. I am writing for lost and suicidal people in their teens and twenties (and maybe older—a good deal older, perhaps), who need to know that it's okay to tell the truth about what has happened to them. Our lives depend on honesty and it is hard-won. It is crazy-making—and I mean that in the full weight of the term—to expect abused people to protect their abusers. It happens all the time. And guess what? Mental illness is on the rise. We need to raise up a generation of truth-tellers to enter into the journey of true healing (for more information, read the afterword).

I didn't talk to Dad for three years as I rediscovered my inner truth: I was a victim, and now I would be a survivor. I think the distance also helped him mature when he realized he couldn't control me. It opened him up to become his best self. He never *wanted* to hurt me. He just didn't respect himself, and therefore didn't respect me, in other words, a part of him. Perhaps the part of him that he loved most deeply. And hated.

He really changed when he lost me as his daughter, though not all daughters are lucky enough for this to be the case. Some dads don't care or exclusively wish their children harm. Some moms or nonbinary parents too. Some people I've talked to say that it may be harder if your parent loves and hates you at the same time. It's more of a mind warp. Regardless, I'm sure this distance was devastating to him, but it became a need. I needed to survive and I was suicidal. Again, one blessing in my life was that he didn't die when we were not interacting with each other, which would have been a regret of mine for the rest of my life. But, regardless, I know I would have literally died without the enforced distance, so I think with time I would have forgiven myself had he died.

It was so confusing to realize I was abused and to grow into that deep inner knowledge I had always had of that fact, and then to have Dad just brush it aside. My therapist at the time was fully supportive. He also wasn't Christian, and I think the two are related. A lot of times in the church, abuse victims are told that they should forgive and forget. I had a friend who was in a severe domestic violence situation who was Christian fundamentalist. Her husband routinely stood up in front of church and "repented" and she was instructed to take him back again and again. This is insanity. Furthermore, true repentance means a "change in heart" in the Bible, which is absolutely about a change in behavior as well. Her husband said he had repented, but really, he was far from it. Eventually she got a divorce and started going to an American fundamentalist church rather than the Slavic one she had been going to. I don't agree with her theologically on all matters, but she is positively radiant and her faith life enriches mine every time I see her.

Justice in relationships is marked by nonviolence, and this means relationships across people groups and our relationship with the planet as well (see my friend Caleb's essay in the appendix). In other words, this includes racial justice. The nonviolence wheel accompanies the violence one and is a companion to it, though I haven't seen it tied to social movement before. But think about this next time you are in a crosscultural interaction. The eight features are as follows:

1. Economic partnership
2. Negotiation and fairness
3. Non-threatening behavior
4. Respect
5. Trust and support

6. Honesty and accountability
7. Responsible parenting
8. Shared responsibility

The hub of the graphic reads "Equality" and the circle surrounding the eight items reads "Nonviolence." In this book I explore the mind, body, soul, and spirit. I conclude with their integration into society. What justice looks like depends on one's social location. My family has had a checkered and yet also, in other ways, uplifting past. My family has had affairs in previous generations, deaths by suicide and alcoholism, severe child neglect, and other misfortunes. This, I find, is common. One great-grandpa was in the KKK in the 1930s, a dark period in the American South, and historically that line of the family enslaved African Americans. Therefore, the royalties for all my books go to racial justice initiatives and endowments related to women's rights and leadership. We have also started several racial justice endowments even though we're not millionaires. What I'm sharing is my path, not yours, so don't think I'm trying to sway you to my side. I do not write for money—it changes how I write to worry about book marketing or earning royalties—and I work hard to write well when I do write. This is not possible for everyone, nor is it appropriate for people who come from marginalized and oppressed communities to start endowments or not be paid for their labor. As a middle-class white person I give sacrificially, and the people who receive our funds deserve to flourish without guilt or strings attached.

People who are abused and recover can spread love and heal intergenerational wounds.

You can break the cycle.

Stephen Covey talks about this as being a "transition person." A transition person disrupts the flow of negativity that can get passed down intergenerationally or situationally. I like to think of myself as a transition person in progress. I can still be negative to others and have, when on less medicine, wounded people emotionally. But this is less and less the case for me, and I'm always improving. I'm committed to my treatment plan, I go to checkups at the doctor's, care for my teeth, get my eyes checked, get mammograms, and try to spend my days as meaningfully and also effectively as possible. My medicine makes that possible. Many people with psychosis struggle with self-care when we are not in treatment and taking good care of ourselves. It's a stereotype, but with care and God's grace, and a good deal of work on myself, I have come to the point of being able to consistently defy that stereotype. I'm sharing this so you have a model of what it looks like to be a familial and a cultural transition person. I run a decolonial Spanish missions website (biblespanish. com) and teach ESL and Spanish informally and, in keeping with decolonial practice, I do this for free.

I have read books by white people on decoloniality, and really, to me, this reads like white people colonizing decoloniality. Really, we need to read books by people of color and culture and let them lead us if we are white people, so I'm not going to wax decolonial here. This has to do with the eight features of nonviolence above. Really think about how these principles are important in families and among diverse people groups.

It is my conviction that familial trauma encourages systemic cultural trauma and that cultural trauma plays out in families.

Healed people heal not just families, but their churches and the world.

> *The Messiah has made things up between us so that we're now together on this, both non-Jewish outsiders and Jewish insiders. He tore down the wall we used to keep each other at a distance. He repealed the law code that had become so clogged with fine print and footnotes that it hindered more than it helped. Then he started over. Instead of continuing with two groups of people separated by centuries of animosity and suspicion, he created a new kind of human being, a fresh start for everybody.*
>
> *Christ brought us together through his death on the cross. The Cross got us to embrace, and that was the end of the hostility. Christ came and preached peace to you outsiders and peace to us insiders. He treated us as equals, and so made us equals. Through him we both share the same Spirit and have equal access to the Father.*

—Eph 2:14–18

Afterword

WHEN I WAS IN a doctoral class a truth hit me that had not dawned on me during my entire life as a Christian and minister to that point. It was so simple and yet so deeply profound and true. I was stunned by how new and revelatory this idea was. How could I have missed this? This little truth then began to open me up to a world that I had glanced at before—but now it captured my gaze with unrelenting passion.

I was blessed to grow up in a very loving Christian home and had attended church my entire life with two wonderful pastors who were thoughtful preachers. I was privileged to have wonderful undergraduate and masters-level theological training. I had been in ministry for over a decade and this insight was like a bolt of lightning that shot through me in a way that left me stunned.

My life in the church, my theological training, and my pastoral ministry had always focused on helping sinners find healing and forgiveness. The classic case study is David who, even though he was a man after God's own heart, had failed miserably with the rape and murder of Bathsheba and Uriah. So the goal of ministry and our communal worship gatherings was to be like the prophet Nathan, to lovingly confront David and to get him to confess his sin. We were to invite him into repentance so he could experience God's healing and forgiveness. Our singing and preaching were focused on inviting sinners to be forgiven. This was the gospel.

Yet the book *The Other Side of Sin* shook me out of this rut. What about the healing and salvation needed by those who have been sinned against? What was the church's ministry in teaching, preaching, and communal worship to those who have been sinned against? How was God to care for and help Bathsheba? What about Uriah, her murdered husband?

That I needed to be intentionally exposed to this thought also testifies to the deep privilege I had been nurtured in. In my early teen years, I woke up to my friend's lives, and like a slow sunrise, I began to gain clarity on how blessed and sheltered my life was. The churches I had attended had only led me to encounters with kids and adults who were kind and loving. Even my time in ministry consisted of blessed days with very little turmoil and struggle. I have no reason to understand why, but people in my life had only been kind, gracious, and loving to me. In this way, I had been raised to be completely ignorant to the experiences of pain, hurt, and betrayal that most experience in their lives.

As I considered the place and situation of the sinned against, the gospel became much more complicated. This basic gospel of sinners finding forgiveness took on a new layer of complexity and God's apparent lack of care for the sinned against. Considering Bathsheba's perspective, God has allowed David to rape her and then have her husband killed. But then after being confronted by Nathan, David confessed his sin and then God had the audacity to forgive David, her abuser and murderer of her husband. Did God care for Bathsheba? Is this gospel really good news for everybody?

While I had rightly been forced to theologically and pastorally consider the problem of theodicy—that a loving and powerful God allows persons to experience evil—I had not considered how the basic gospel message is perhaps not good news for the victims of sin.

In this same season I also learned about the Asian concept of *han*. *Han* considers carefully the danger when persons have been hurt and wounded by others. *Han* names the plight of those who have been sinned against. Moreover, it did give a theological framework for the often-used phrase *hurt people, hurt people*. In thinking about the pastoral ministry I had both sat under and then performed I came to be aware that often the response given to the sinned against were often providing another layer of injury. It was often a combination of "I am so sorry you were hurt. Remember Jesus said you need to forgive people if you want God to forgive you. And by the way remember that Rom 3:23 says that all of us have sinned, so maybe just focus on the things you have done wrong as a way of finding healing."

As I reflect on this now, while there was not any intention to hurt those who were victims of others' sins, this was and is simply pastoral abuse. While certainly, forgiveness and confessions of sin is appropriate for all persons, much more care and theological wisdom must be employed.

So where is God?

Jürgen Moltmann in his powerful book, *The Crucified God*, proclaims powerfully and prophetically that in the life, death, and crucifixion of Jesus, the triune God enters into the very place of God-forsakenness—God does not stop evil from wreaking havoc upon the innocent. Yet in the life and crucifixion of Jesus, embodied in the cry of lament on the cross, God enters into God-forsakenness. So now there is no place that can be called godforsaken.

Where is God in the midst of the sinned-against's pain, despair, and isolation, weeping, and lamenting?

God is there with that person.

Certainly, it is true that forgiveness is God's desire in all situations. However, when dealing with an intensity of those who are being sinned against, the perpetrator does not get to decide the timeline for how this forgiveness is sought and offered.

It is true that forgiveness for both the sinner and the sinned-against can set people free from acts of abuse, pain, and exploitation. When someone is sinned-against they have been violated and disempowered. Part of the healing of forgiveness is empowering them, awakening them to the reality that they are in charge of the timeline for if and when forgiveness will be offered.

Demanding quick forgiveness of the perpetrator is, again, pastoral abuse. For some situations the intensity of abuse may mean that this process takes years.

It is also important to remember the goal of forgiveness. Forgiveness is not a control-alt-delete—it is not an undoing of the sin and it is not pretending as if nothing has happened. As Easter is not an undoing of Jesus' crucifixion, but rather is about new life that breaks the power of death, so forgiveness hopes to offer the sinner and the sinned-against a place of new life after the evil has occurred. As with the resurrected Christ, the scars of sin will always remain.

For the sinned-against, it is very possible that the road to forgiveness always leaves scars. Forgiveness hopes that the scars do not hold the victim captive to their abuser or the events of abuse. Similarly, in many cases forgiveness and reconciliation do not mean even that a relationship continues. For some victims, forgiveness and reconciliation and healing may simply mean they do not wish their perpetrator a vicious and painful death. Every situation is unique, and God's healing is powerful, but more attention and care must be given to the sinned-against than has been done thus far in the church. While it is true that some victims do get stuck in the process, pastors should work with and defer to counselors to help victims moving toward healing from the abuse.

Another way the church can better care for and shepherd persons who have experienced trauma and been sinned against is through communal worship, singing, preaching, and sacraments. To begin, communal worship must recover the powerful practice of lament. Too often, lament has been ignored and forgotten. Lament is worship, a worship of protest, expressing anger at God for not having prevented this event from happening. Additionally, lament entails crying out in a place of honest despair, pain, and challenge. If authentic lament is not given space in communal worship, the contrived worship of praise is simply dishonest. Also, in teaching, preaching, and praying, space must be given to hear and name how devastating it is to hurt another human being. The sinner and sinned against need to publicly proclaim, and hear, an honest reckoning of the intensity of damage wrought by sinning against someone.

When the gospel is offered with simple and quick forgiveness, the gospel has been neglected. Moreover, when forgiveness is simply me saying I am sorry to God for hurting Sam, but I never approach Sam, this is also not the gospel and Jesus clearly teaches the opposite. Yet even as I approach Sam seeking forgiveness there must not be any demand or timeline by me, the perpetrator, for a response. Again, underneath both the erasure of lament and the verticalization of sin—whereby we just seek forgiveness from God rather than from our victims—the church's worship has been focused on the powerful victimizers and the sinned-against have been ignored. We can do better.

Considering *han* again, if a pastor simply dismisses a person's wounds and tells them just to focus on the ways they have sinned, this is tantamount to putting a Band-Aid on cancer. Say a man, Charlie, was abused as a child. If he abuses children as an adult, this is *never* to be rationalized as OK. However, Charlie needs to deal with his *han*; *han* will work itself out either redemptively or destructively. Inviting Charlie to work on his painful and abused past is not a quick fix, but simply names that our bodies remember the abuse and it must be attended to.

So how does this relate to persons who have not only been traumatized and abused but also those who suffer with mental illness? Every person's journey is unique. Certainly, some mental illness can be a result of past abuse and trauma. It can also be a result of genetics, or it simply comes via chemical imbalances or a variety of factors where no one or thing is culpable.

Unfortunately, just as pastoral abuse around the victims of sin occurs, so, too, the church has not done well when persons with mental illness are entrusted to their care. *While it should not need to be said, mental illness does not remain because people lack faith or don't trust God to heal.* Moreover, God can use science, counseling, and medicine to help people. It is hopeful that persons are taking their mental health seriously and no longer have to hide in the shadows of shame. Every person and journey is different, but the church must create space to love, care, and nurture those who face the journey of mental illness. While the church should pray for mental health and peace, in the grand lamentable mystery of life, some find respite and others do not. In the spirit of Rom 12:15, we rejoice with those who rejoice and mourn with those who mourn.

Erin Grimm, with gentle humility, has invited us into her journey. She does so not to promote an awkward voyeurism, but rather as a way to open up the unique journey many face that has too often been ignored by the church and the larger society. One of the great pains for many is feeling isolated and believing one's experience is not understood or shared by anyone else. They are often very alone.

The great saying in Christian history is that the church is reformed and always needing to be reformed. May God help those who have felt invisible in their pain, find a beam of light from Christians who don't have easy answers but just desire to be present with those on the journey.

Let us remember especially in the case of those who struggle with trauma, mental illness, or who have been sinned against that, as Christians (and humans), we are our each other's keepers. With all those whom God brings across our path, may we take the time to be present.

May those who find a great deal of connection with Erin's journey, or who have found themselves in distress and pain, find a community of love and embrace to journey with them. God is not against them. God is present with them in their joy and in their pain. May the church also be.

Brent Peterson, PhD
Nampa, Idaho
April 19, 2023

Appendix

Appendix

Heart Breath Meditation

By Lita Artis, LMT, Erin's Massage Therapist

This meditation piece is inspired by HeartMath® and Polyvagal Theory.

ONE OF THE MOST kind and compassionate acts of self-care is to breathe through our heart space. A simple practice of a slowing and deepening our breath can not only get us out of our heads and into our bodies, it can also reset our nervous system to move one into a more relaxed state.

In scientific terms this practice establishes a coherency between our hearts and our brains via the electromagnetic relationship between the two.

The technique is simple:

Place your hands in the center of your chest, or even over your heart which lies just to the left of the center of your chest. Breathe in and out of your heart space.

Breathe in and out with a sense of ease, comfort, peace, and softness.

See if you can bring balance to the length of the in-breath to that of the out-breath, a few seconds on the inhale, a few seconds on the exhale. Can you hold this pattern of breathing for fifteen seconds, one minute, or five minutes? Our minds can wander easily, but with a simple suggestion we can go back to this breathing in and out of the heart.

When I engage in this practice, I like to notice what happens. Initially, under my hands as they rest on my heart, I become aware of how shallow my breath is or how tired I am. I then feel some warmth arise in my chest and the beginnings of an energetic connection between my heart and my hands. And what follows is an interesting cascade of sensations. My heart space opens up. I can feel my shoulders relax, my breath becomes deeper, and the business and busyness of my mind slows down.

Five minutes of this breath assists to balance the nervous system, supports our immune system, reduces blood pressure, supports "bigger mind" decision-making, and rebalances the body and emotions following periods of stress, anger, or anxiety.

If you/we add an emotion of gratitude or appreciation as you do this practice, an expansion of our electromagnetic field occurs. The simple infusion of a memory of someone, something, or some experience for which we are grateful amplifies this field and can influence the larger space around us.

So simple and potent this practice is, and it comes with a package of benefits, so to speak. It is free. You can do it anytime, anywhere. I sometimes do this at night in bed when my mind is racing. I will often use three breaths for each of my loved ones, and I can't even get through three or four people before I am asleep. This is my experience. You may experience something else.

Decolonizing Creation

By Caleb Cray Haynes

Then God said, "Let us make humans in our image, according
to our likeness, and let them have dominion over the fish of
the sea and over the birds of the air and over the cattle and
over all the wild animals of the earth and over every creeping
thing that creeps upon the earth."

—Gen 1:26

It's perhaps providential that I would connect with Erin. In
her work here, Erin shares her story, and I think if we are willing to
see it, we will all find windows into our own stories and even pat-
terned within creation. The movement of colonization to decolo-
nization, from trauma to healing, from slavery to liberation is the
story of the people of God, and I would argue all of creation.

Erin writes, "Justice in relationships is marked by nonviolence." I believe this also reflects our relationship with the Earth.
Creation has suffered intergenerational trauma since *the fall* in Gen
3 and, as Paul asserts in Rom 8:18–25, creation groans as it awaits
the freedom of the glory of the children of God! In the essay "Jesus Is Coming—Plant a Tree," acclaimed theologian N. T. Wright
argues that this is not distant future glory, but rather one that is
presently alive and at work.

To begin seeing our relationship with creation this way is challenging if you've never peered behind that particular curtain before. But it's no coincidence that what follows Gen 3 is a set of falling dominos between humanity and creation as we are exiled from paradise, brother murders brother, blood cries out from the ground, and great sin precedes great floods that ravage the earth. By Gen 11, humanity is building great towers in order to push past its own limitations into the heavens. Since that first bite of forbidden fruit we've been assuming we can consume whatever we want, however we want, whenever we want. Is this what God had in mind when we were given the gift of "dominion?"

In the English language the close connection between the term "dominion," used in the Bible to describe human's relationship to the planet and its creatures, and "domination" has offered nothing short of theological confusion. God offers us a holy vocation within creation and, given our fallen state, it's no surprise that we find ourselves interpreting dominion as domination.

A closer look at Gen 1 (and the entire arc of Scripture) reveals that God's creative work within creation has never been human-centric (or what scholars call "anthropocentric," *anthro* meaning human). The Genesis creation poem is beautiful, containing within itself deep truths about where we are, who we are, and what we're doing here. Genesis tells us that God spends the first few days creating three spaces or containers: the sky, the water, and the land. The next three days God fills those spaces up with stars, birds, fish, squid, cattle and creepy-crawlies! God creates containers and then fills each container with its appropriate things. The containers reveal to us the nature of the life that exist within that particular container, and also the life within informs us of the nature of the container. So far so good!

But at the end of the last creating day God seems to be wrapping things up when a kind of crescendo occurs. In Gen 1:26, God says, "Let us make humankind in our image, according to our likeness; and let them have dominion over the fish of the sea, and over the birds of the air, and over the cattle, and over all the wild animals of the earth, and over every creeping thing that creeps upon the earth."

This is where we get into trouble: we attempt to interpret dominion through the lens of domination, rather than of service and love. This kind of translation is highly problematic as it stands in direct contradiction to who we come to know our God to be throughout Scripture, especially within the person of Jesus! Jesus's rule looks like loving relationality, mutuality, authenticity, and laying your life down for the other. Knowing Christ, how could we understand the posture of dominion in any other way?

In fact, centuries ago, the theologian Thomas Aquinas even spoke about how "dominion" is shaped by charity. *It is only through love that we can know what dominion is.* Creation in Gen 1 occurs pre *the fall*, thus, *before* sin, greed and so on . . . Therefore, dominion cannot be synonymous with an oppressive rule. Creation simply does not exist to orbit around the needs and consumption of humanity, but scandalously, the opposite:

> *Humanity is given the holy responsibility of working to serve creation.*

In his book of essays, *What Are People for?*, farmer, writer, and poet Wendell Berry states that the Bible teaches us that, ecologically, God created the world because God wanted to. God calls the world good and loves it. It is God's world. He has never given it to humans, Berry reminds us. We are tasked to take care of it, Berry continues, because, "If God loves the world, then how might any person of faith be excused for not loving it or justified in destroying it?"

How might the people of God lead the way toward global ecological well-being? As we seek to live into our original God-ordered relationship with all creation and follow our Savior, Jesus, who is already about "the reconciliation of all things"—see Col 1:20—we will offer freedom to creation. And we shouldn't be surprised that as we work toward the liberation of all creation from the grip of greed, good news will be brought to the poor, the captive will go free, those who are blind will find sight, the oppressed will find freedom, and God's coming kingdom on earth will be hastened.

Rev. Caleb Cray Haynes is the director of Nazarenes for Creation Care and an ordained elder in the Church of the Nazarene. He serves as the community & creation pastor at Kaleo Nashville Church of the Naza-rene and is a partner with the Evangelical Environmental Network. Caleb is also the author of Garbage Theology: The Unseen World of Waste and What It Means for the Salvation of Every Person, Every Place, and Every Thing.

A Hopeful Lens for Those Who Choose to Adopt

The Adoption Journey

By Stacie Latimer

Twenty-five years ago, my husband and I got on a plane, headed to Chennai, India to meet the beautiful little girl who was to become our daughter. Kala.

Kala—the eighteen-month-old who stole our hearts at the very first photos we were given. Kala—for whom we'd completed piles of paperwork . . . fingerprints and bank statements and interviews and letters recommending us as parents. Kala. To whom we'd sent *Goodnight Moon* and pajamas . . . awaiting every new picture and update. Kala. For whom we'd waited a grueling eight months for this moment. For whom we could nearly hear her childhood ticking away.

Kala spent her first twenty-six months of life in the Foundling Home in Chennai. Here, she shared space and resources with approximately twenty-seven other very young children. We admire and deeply respect the small, dedicated staff and their care for the children, but given limited resources and personnel, a child's experience is still that of an orphanage.

We walked up four flights of stairs, carefully walking past disabled children in the stairwell, unsure of where we were headed or how this was to happen. We knew only that she was on the top floor and that in the space of the next few minutes, all of our lives were about to change forever.

We took off our shoes on the top floor. Three small rooms and many beautiful little faces—one of whom was quickly plucked up and placed in my arms. Kala. I somehow thought there would be a ceremony—something—but this was so overwhelmingly sudden and real. All I could do is sob, look at her, and repeat, "It's you. It's you." She bravely left the world she'd known and began her adjustments to a new and very different world.

Five years later we began the journey again, to the same foundling home—this time to meet and bring "home" our son, Apoorva (now Liam), at twenty-four months of age.

Kala is now twenty-seven years old, and Liam is twenty-two. Kala has her college degree, Liam is in pursuit of his. We have had bumps and bruises along the way—life is life—but it's been such immense privilege to be their mom. My life has been enriched, challenged and expanded in ways I couldn't put into words.

Adoption has been in my life since sixth grade and beyond, as two sets of cousins and my sister all have adopted (both domestically and internationally). Adopting became even more of a desire of mine as I volunteered for three months in an orphanage in Braila, Romania in 1991. (If you are old enough to remember, the images you saw of the conditions were accurate. The human part of the story and Ceausescu's part in it all were likely not accurate.)

My view of adoption and the ethics of the process were expanded and clarified as I returned from Romania and began working for an international child welfare and adoption agency: the World Association for Children and Parents. In WACAP's statement of purpose, it reads, "We are finding families for children, not children for families." This is an important distinction about how the adoption process should be viewed and practiced, and insures the rights of the triad in adoption—birth mother, child, and adoptive parent. It's why I jumped careers to join them.

And while my own, my family's, and extended family's experiences led me toward international adoption, my personal social justice focus, especially as a public school teacher, has led me to do some deep reflection around the needs of children in foster care. I must call this out in any writing about adoption. (There are currently over 391,000 children and youth in foster care in the US.)[1]

Because I am challenged here to write about adoption, I will move for a moment away from the personal and bullet point a few things about parenthood—via birth or adoption—which to me, are primary considerations.

> In becoming a parent, via birth or adoption, there are just no guarantees. Not for a future fulfilled that one always imagined, or regarding the health/disposition of the child. Because we know more about a child waiting for a family if adopting, questions can be asked that wouldn't be able to be answered of a baby in utero. This can be uncomfortable at best. It is a child we're talking about, in need of a family, not a purchase or transaction . . . but asking about family history, medical concerns, etc. is common sense. I just hope it's not looked at as any extra guarantee of health or how a family might "be."

> Building a family in many ways becomes . . . building a family. If the focus is centered on the child being the center, the things which may be "swirling" about (struggles with infertility, for example) may be seen in a different light. Both are a process. Adoption is a different journey if ability to have a birth child isn't in the cards. It isn't a replacement or distraction from the possible grief of infertility. That said, if parents are prepared and committed to providing a home for a child, ready to meet the needs and challenges, embrace the joys and growth, a child that comes to you via adoption is truly your own. In deep and profound ways.

> Adoption may have some extra "glow." This might include that of being a "forever home" that might not have occurred for a child (especially for older or medically fragile or challenged children domestically or internationally). A glow that within your own family and in fellow adoptive families, you get to be privy to the resilience

1. See "Key Facts and Statistics" at https://www.childwelfare.gov/fostercaremonth/awareness/facts/.

of children who adjust and so often, thrive. A glow that if internationally adopting, you are offered the privilege of connection to another country and culture. (This comes with the responsibility to offer as much connection for the child as you can.) A glow that you feel connected to families who have adopted, and have a "honed" heart for issues around children who are vulnerable and may face the extra challenges adoption may bring (attachment disorder, identity questions).

The process can be heartbreaking and expensive, again depending on domestic or international, and the choices you make around adoption: age, gender, possible medical risks or disabilities. An ethical agency will connect you with a child after knowing your choices and with full disclosure and recommendation that you contact your family physician. And allow you time to process—without judgement. There can't be many processes in life more important or "weighted" than bringing together children with families.

Adoption may not be a "smooth" path. International adoptions rely on governments, policies, and events which may change how or even if adoptions can continue. If domestic, birth parents may change their mind or re-enter a child's life. The trauma of a child suffering abuse or neglect may rise greater than the love and commitment you're there to offer. Or at least challenge both.

There is much more to say, and the information is readily available, so I will go back to the very personal. I have to end on the very "human" part of this total experience.

For me, and many adoptive parents I know, the bonding process was as solid as having a waxy infant placed on your stomach. The "rightness" of you being together as family lands solidly in "meant to be."

Each time (still!) my children casually say, "Mom! Can you . . . ?" or "Mom! Guess what?" it is an honor. It was honor to meet two beautiful women in saris who cared for my children for their first two years of life, and who worked tirelessly in every step of our adoption process and time in India. It is an honor to answer curious questions (mostly just curious) about what your family "looks like" or what it is to adopt. It is the biggest honor, having walked alongside my children at soccer practice and dance recitals and birthday parties and Girl Scouts—and more recently, job interviews and Army boot camp.

I end with a deep bow to parents of all kinds, families of all kinds, and all children for their courage. I end with a hope that each child can go to sleep assured and loved, knowing that tomorrow will feel just like today.

Thank you for reading my thoughts.

The First Chapter of
the Book of James

Why I Translated This.
Aren't There Enough Versions?

EVERYTHING I DO IN life as a Christian is based off the first chapter of the book of James. I would never have rededicated my life to Christ as an adult if it weren't for my knowledge of other languages. My Russian and Ukrainian friends had a simpler and purer faith, uncompromised by forays into science or historical criticism. They advised me not to take my mental health medication, and I almost died from the mental health episode that followed. But while worshipping with them, a deeper essence of Christianity also emerged from the depths of their provincialism and I reconnected with God in a way that had never been possible after my education in the secular humanities. I wanted to share their perspective with you, filtered through my own perspective on the Bible when experienced reading alongside them.

There is so much baggage that comes with reading the Bible in English. To name a few things: colonialism, nationalist fundamentalism, trans/homophobia. These things are found in other cultures as well, but for some reason, reading the Bible in Russian *as a progressive American* feels like home. So, I thought I would share this with you. Please read it carefully. You may find that Christianity breathes again when you do.

WHO WROTE THE BOOK OF JAMES?
AND DOES IT MATTER?

There are so many different takes on the Bible and the history of how it was written. Sadly, the way people identify themselves in terms of politics can also shape what they see as true of the Bible. It should not be this way.

The way I like to frame it is as follows:

The book of James was written by Jesus's brother (same mother, obviously different father—Joseph—since Jesus is the Son of God).

James ministered to the Jews of the diaspora. Diaspora means spread out. Dispersed.

The Jews had converted to Christianity but were dispersed as a result of persecution on account of their Christianity. When we make the change for Christ in our lives, we will come under attack. James teaches us how to stand firm.

JAMES 1:1–8

Wisdom, faith, and the plight of the double-souled:

> Beloved twelve tribes of Israel, who have been scattered amongst various peoples: I, James, a servant of God and the Lord Jesus Christ, greet you affectionately. Siblings, when you are coming up against various difficult experiences life brings, consider it to be a great joy. You know that such trials of faith yield endurance, and that such endurance should grow up mightily, and to such a great degree, that you would become, once and for all, mature (as great orchards or wise elders); in other words, you will become integrated, integrous, without any shortcoming whatsoever. If any of you has insufficient wisdom, simply ask God, who, without reproaching us, generously gives of it—you will indeed receive wisdom!
>
> The person who asks for it, however, must truly believe, not in the least bit doubting, because those who doubt resemble the waves of the sea, carried about and shattered by the wind. No such person should count on receiving anything whatsoever from the LORD. Such a person

*is double-souled and lacks strength in every single thing
that they do.*

Analysis

This was at first difficult to read for me as a woman with a mental
health condition. While I don't doubt in terms of faith—I have total
faith in God—I often have a schizophrenic doubleness in life and have
pursued tangents that led nowhere because I wasn't fully integrated
when I made important decisions. Study this passage often and you
will grow in wisdom and will make more informed decisions.

JAMES 1:9–11

Think twice if you're proud to be rich and distinguished:

> *The sibling of the lower class, in fact, can brag on account
> of their high position. And the rich person can brag about
> their lowliness, because they will vanish like a wildflower.
> The sun rises and with its heat it dries up the plant, its
> flower falls off, and all of its beauty fades. In exactly this
> way, even the rich person will wilt and die in the midst of
> their endeavors.*

Analysis

Things are not always what they seem. Throughout the Old and
New Testaments, the lowly are made high and the high made low.
Wealth and power often bring corruption, especially dishonest
wealth, including wealth from racial oppression and discrimination
such as that perpetrated against minorities.

Parallel text (Acts 10:28–29):

> *Peter said to them: "You yourselves know that Jews are
> forbidden from socializing with non-Jews or entering their
> homes. But God showed me that I should call no person*

unholy or unclean, and therefore, when you came to bring me here, I left to see you without objection."

JAMES 1:12–18

On temptation and the nature of God:

Blessed is the person who carries on in the face of difficult times, enduring them to the very end. Such a person will receive the crown of life that God promised to all who love Godself. When temptation overtakes you, do not say, "It's God who's tempting me." God Godself cannot be tempted by evil and God tempts no one. Each person is tempted by their very own personal desires; they distract and seduce the person. Then desire conceives and births sin, and the committed sin gives birth to death itself. My dear, dear siblings, do not go off the beaten path and lose yourselves. All good and perfect gifts are brought forth from above, from the Creator of Lights, in whom there is no change or alteration whatsoever. God Godself, by God's very own will, birthed us with the word of Truth, so that it would fall to us to be the first fruits of God's creatures.

Analysis

Notice that it says *when* temptation overtakes us, not *if*. We will be tempted, but we do always have the choice in how to respond. In this way we can preserve dignity even in our profound humanity.

JAMES 1:19–27

What kind of drinker are you?

My dear siblings, I implore you to understand that each of us should be more inclined to listen than to speak or display anger. In anger people don't do anything of use to God. Therefore, abandon all impurity and all traces of evil and, in gentleness, partake of the ingrafted, implanted Word that has the power to save your souls.

At the same time, be not only listeners of the Word, but be also fulfillers of it, otherwise you're just deceiving yourselves. Whoever listens to the Word but doesn't fulfill it is like one who looks in the mirror: they examine themselves, walk away, and instantly forget how they look. But the person who continually and invariably immerses themself in the Perfect Law, the Law which gives freedom, and enters into harmony with it, not forgetting about what they have heard, will be blessed in their endeavors. Whoever considers themselves pious and yet cannot control their tongue, is deceiving themselves, and the piety of such a person is of no use. Clean and pure piety before God consists in helping orphans and widows in their needs and keeping oneself cleansed of the world.

Analysis

I have noticed that some Christians are so set on not being "those kinds of holiness Christians" that they see it as almost spiritual to drink, often to the point of intoxication. They are like children who are learning that their parents weren't perfect and who run further away from sobriety with each passing year.

Parallel verse:

> *Be vigilant and wakeful. Your enemy, the devil, roams all around you, like a roaring lion in search of a victim. Be strong in faith and resist the devil, understanding that all over the world your siblings endure similar sufferings.* (1 Pet 5:8–9)

Fact

The holiness movement is traditionally associated with avoidance of alcohol. This is because it arose in the nineteenth century, when strong liquor rather than light beer became the standard fare. People didn't understand the risk of alcoholism because they had formerly been able to drink amply without adverse effects. Significant social ills resulted from the profound alcoholism that ensued, and Christians realized to combat sin, they had to address its source of the era: strong drink. Overly zealous religious people often have addictive personalities. Alcoholism is a leading cause of death in Russian men. That and suicide. The average lifespan is mid-fifties for men on account of drink and suicide. Mental health treatment is extremely stigmatized in Russia and so a lot of people self-medicate, which is dangerous and unnecessary. When we live with psychosis it is important to avoid over-relying on drugs and alcohol. I avoid them completely.

From the Forthcoming
Nine Principles of Hope: On Making a Difference as a Christian

I INITIALLY WROTE THIS book for myself. Its writing began while I was still working toward publishing my first book, *Emergent Grace*, in 2022. I was so proud of myself and really thought that I had arrived at my maturity, as I had written about how to live with maturity as a person with mental illness; but then, as so often happens, I realized my own hypocrisy when it came to living out what I had written. Don't get me wrong, I had grown leaps and bounds since when I was in my twenties and would swear, shout, slam the door, and run around the block or drive away (much to my husband's confusion, since he was raised in a calm household).

"I am better now!" I had thought to myself.

I placed in the appendix of *Emergent Grace* the outline of the principles I share in this book and some relevant Bible verses. I had developed those principles out of conscious comparison between Buddhism and Christianity while I was a Buddhist Christian. Buddhist frameworks calmed me when I was having a hard time, while Christian ones proved overstimulating, anxiety-producing, and upsetting, triggering a downward spiral with their constant striving for excellence and joy. Over time, however, I realized that there was considerable overlap between some of the main principles of mindfulness and what Jesus teaches and exemplifies, with the central difference being that Christianity centers on hope, while Buddhism is about acceptance. When I realized that, my ability to cope with my serious mental illness grew exponentially, increasing my quality of life and my will to live in the first place. It dawned on me that I could make a difference with my story, so I published a book on living with serious mental illness as a Christian, which was downloaded over three thousand times, and which I finally published with a real publisher in 2023.

I wrote my first book in 2020, but when I finished it, I wasn't sure what to do next in order to be the Christian I was in the book in real life.

"What book should I read," I asked myself, "to really improve my Christian walk in a way that looks like *Jesus* and not just 'me at church,' whatever that means?" In other words, "How can I live a hopeful, helpful, sacrificial, selfless life, without being depressed that I'm not always free from suffering?"

Deep down what I really wanted was calm and peace, which Buddhism had nailed perfectly, while still living in full *engagement* with the real world, a world filled with suffering. Buddhism starts with acceptance of suffering and surrenders to it through non-attachment. I would embrace this and then become less suicidal, but then I would also lack hope. Christian hope would be replaced with dejection, resignation, or a sense of abandonment. I lacked purpose.

I searched my shelves and couldn't find a single book on living Christianly while suffering that wasn't already immersed in the Christian headspace which, when I'm depressed, makes me really unhappy to be Christian. I had books on Christian meditation, books on fruit of the spirit, books on vices and virtues, and so on. But none of them taught me the posture I had learned and functioned so well with as a Buddhist Christian several years ago, before returning to Christianity and acquiring the hope I needed to thrive with my mental health condition. I didn't have any enduring framework for accessing the fruit of the spirit that is the crown jewel of responsible Christian living except for trying to pray and conjure up faith. That was so vague though.

What I needed was a lens through which I would interpret that Bible and the fullness of a Christian life, a life marked by serving others and a sense of dignity and self-worth.

"Isn't it nice to feel loved and lovable by God?" I asked myself, almost willing that sentiment into reality by merely humoring the thought. That's what I wanted more of. And then I realized I was blessed with people in my life who value me, themselves, and others, and who have a lot of wisdom and experience that I don't have. They have blind spots, we all do, but I wanted to focus on the areas where they shined. So, then I decided to interview them and write my own thoughts on the matter alongside their thoughts and reflections so I could turn to those rather than to Buddhism when I felt down. And now it is a whole book. Brief and concise, and yet thick in wisdom, which is what matters most. The fruit of the principles of hope in your life is embodied, rooted Christlikeness.

Made in United States
North Haven, CT
29 August 2023

40883721R00075